THE MAKING OF DAVID MCCOSH

Early Paintings, Drawings, and Prints

July 23 – September 4, 2011

Danielle M. Knapp
McCosh Fellow Curator

Jordan Schnitzer Museum of Art
University of Oregon, Eugene

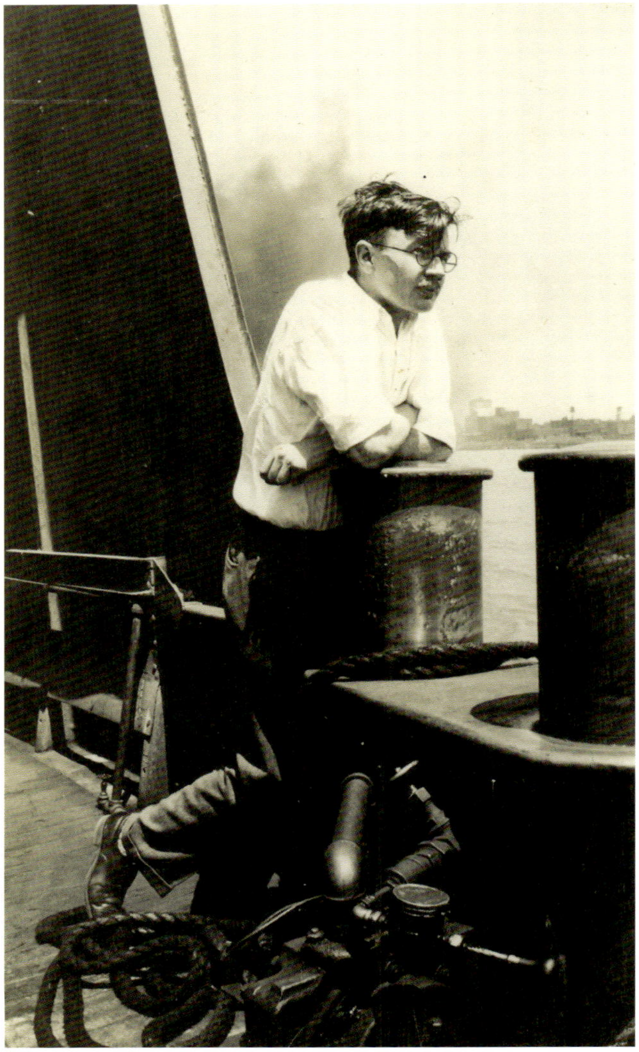

Photo of David McCosh, undated
David John McCosh Memorial Archive
Gift of Anne Kutka McCosh

TABLE OF CONTENTS

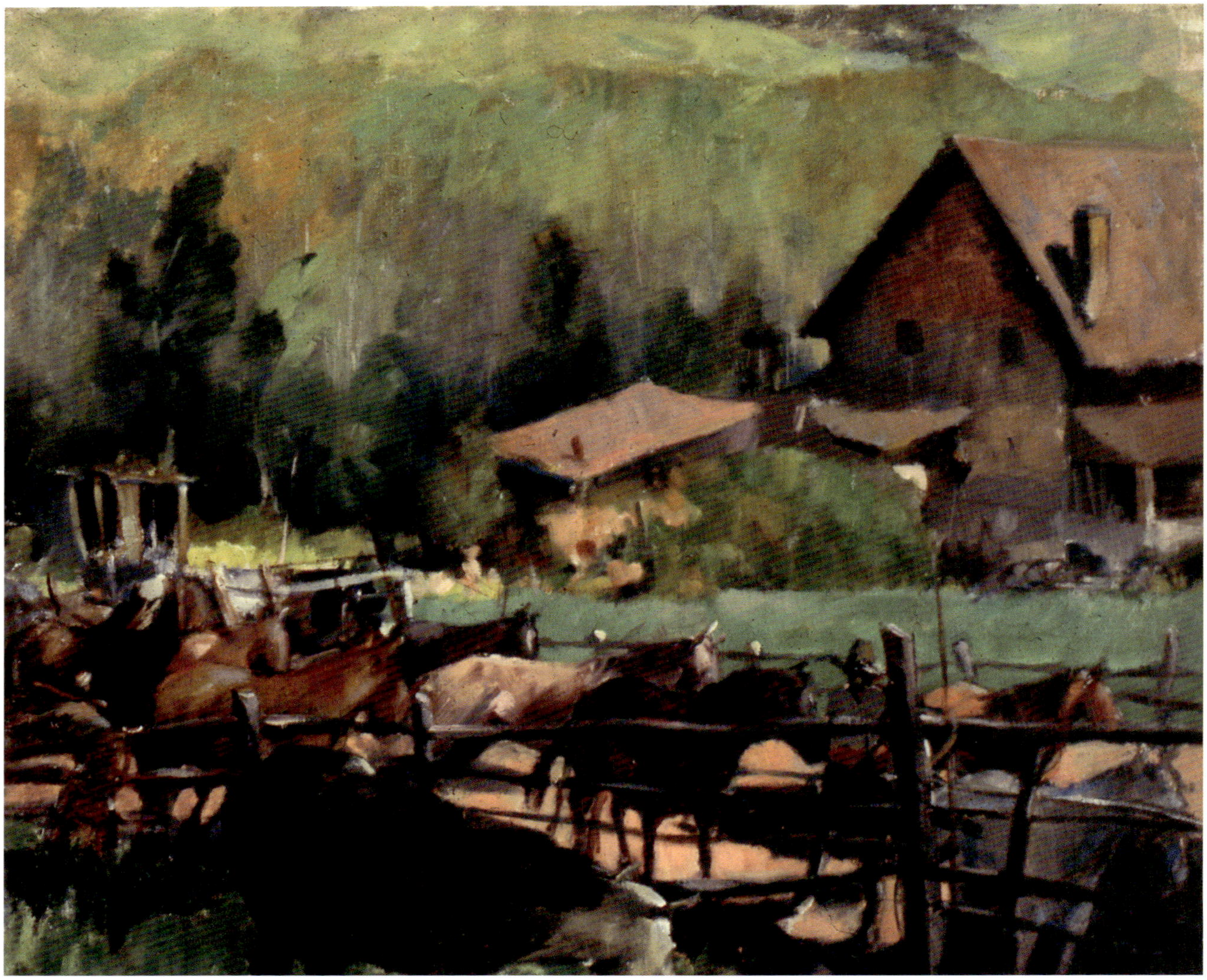

Wyoming, 1927
Oil on linen, 25 x 29 inches
David John McCosh Memorial Collection

David McCosh has an enduring legacy at the Jordan Schnitzer Museum of Art—and rightfully so. Along with more than 170 works by McCosh in the permanent collection, his is one of two artist archives the museum has accepted, the other comprising the largest public collection of works by Morris Graves. Museums think long and hard about accepting such gifts: they create a long-term responsibility, not just for the care of objects, which can range from artworks to letters, photographs, and more, but because they become the primary appreciator and publicist of that person's work and value. Anne Kutka McCosh, the artist's widow, knew this when she entrusted the museum with the McCosh collection and archive and provided generous support for it to pursue these roles through a special endowment.

When McCosh died in 1981, he had lived in Oregon and taught at the University of Oregon for nearly fifty years. As Danielle M. Knapp, McCosh Fellow Curator, details in her essay, McCosh came to the Pacific Northwest well-trained in artistic techniques and art history, but he produced a body of work here that defined his reputation and influenced countless students and colleagues, a number of whom became professional artists, critics, curators, and collectors.

Perhaps, then, it is not surprising that this is the first major exhibition to examine the artist's early work. The museum and the Karin Clarke Gallery, in Eugene, have primarily focused their past exhibitions on the artist's later achievements, and there remains much to explore still in the range of subjects and styles of the Oregon years. But who was McCosh before he came west, what were his artistic influences, and what can we learn from that seminal period of his life and development? In shedding light on this period, Ms Knapp offers substantial historical information and provides new perspectives and suggestions that enhance our understanding of his interests, discipline, and creativity. Perhaps for the first time we are invited to see the young artist in his own right and, in doing so, are better able to connect his developing sensibilities and craft with his older self.

An exceptional graduate from the University of Oregon's MA program in art history, whose research interests focused on the art of the Northwest, Ms Knapp became the museum's first McCosh Fellow Curator following a national search last year. This newly created position of a two-to-three year duration furthers our role as a teaching museum. Not only does the Jordan Schnitzer Museum of Art engage undergraduate and graduate students from a wide range of academic disciplines in internships and employment throughout our operation, but through the creation of the McCosh curatorial fellowship we model our intention to mentor recent art history graduates dedicated to museum careers. We are deeply grateful to The David John McCosh and Anne Kutka McCosh Memorial Museum Endowment Fund and its advisory committee for their support of this position and the exhibition as well as their guidance and commentaries.

Jill Hartz, *Executive Director*

ACKNOWLEDGMENTS

I wish to express my gratitude to Bonnie McCosh, Sandra McCosh Leonard, and the University of Oregon Foundation for making this exhibition and catalog possible; Margaret Coe and the members of the McCosh Advisory Committee—Craig Cheshire, Mark Clarke, Robert Fraser, Hope Pressman, and Roger Saydack—for their dedication to this project and help at all stages of exhibition planning and catalog writing; Ken Kato, Jacob Bartruff, Justin White, and Dana Maher of the InfoGraphics Lab at the University of Oregon for their excellent work in creating digital versions of selections from David McCosh's sketchbooks; Kristy Raine, Mary Helen Burnham, Colleen Thomas, and Jessica Wilks for enthusiastically sharing their research; Matthew Collins, Peter Edberg, Bryna Goodman, Lee Michels, and Jim Walker for their support of this exhibition; Karin Clarke and the wonderful staff of the Karin Clarke Gallery; Vincent and Nan Chapin Arcilesi, Jon Jay Cruson, Dorothy Gilmore, Carl Niederer, Erik Sandgren and Kathryn Cotnoir, and Harry and Mardy Widman for their many kindnesses; and my husband, Chris Knapp, and my family and friends for their love and encouragement.

I am deeply indebted to my colleagues at the Jordan Schnitzer Museum of Art and the University of Oregon: Jill Hartz, executive director, for her inspiring leadership and support of my work as the McCosh Fellow Curator; Anne Rose Kitagawa, chief curator, for her guidance and commitment to excellence; Lawrence Fong, curator of American and regional art, for many years of mentorship and insight; Adriane Tafoya, collections manager, and Gretchen Ranger, registrar, for overseeing the care of the artwork in this exhibition; Kurt Neugebauer, associate director, and Christy McMannis, financial services coordinator, for their help with logistics at every step of the process; Diane Nelson, design services coordinator, for her superb design of this catalog; Charly Swing, chief preparator, Rebecca Urlacher, preparator, and others of the prep staff for their tireless efforts; Jonathan Smith, collection database coordinator, and Malina Graves, photographer, for their beautiful photography; Josh Chadwick, facility and technology manager, for his creative collaboration; Debbie Williamson-Smith, communications coordinator, for her matchless enthusiasm; Emily Kersten, development assistant, Sharon Kaplan, museum educator, Lauren Suveges, administrative and education assistant, and Ashley Gibson, art history graduate student, for their camaraderie and positive reinforcements over the last year; and especially brilliant curatorial interns and art history graduate students June Irene Koehler and Aleksandra Globig for their time, efforts, and level of commitment to this project.

Most of all, I humbly offer my thanks to the late Anne Kutka McCosh for her great foresight and generosity in establishing The David John McCosh and Anne Kutka McCosh Memorial Museum Endowment Fund in 1990.

Danielle M. Knapp, *McCosh Fellow Curator*

The Making of David McCosh

Early Paintings, Drawings, and Prints

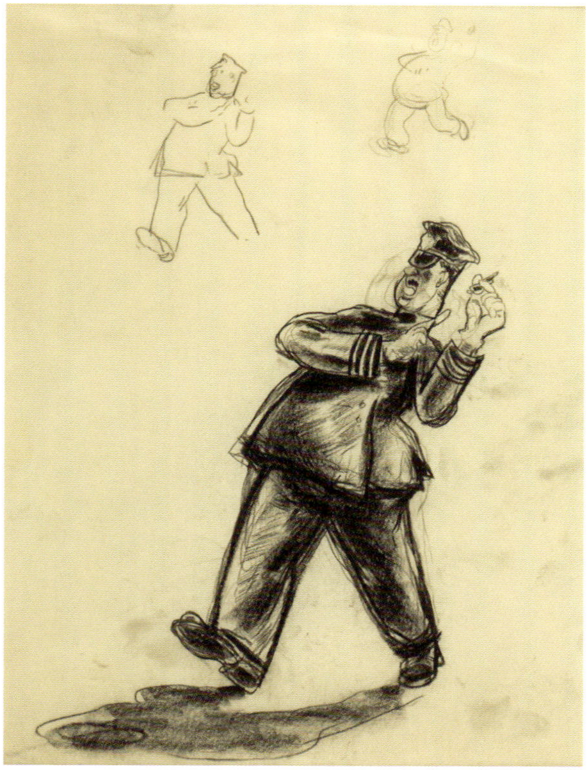

Policeman, n.d.
Charcoal and graphite on paper, 11 x 8½ inches
David John McCosh Memorial Collection

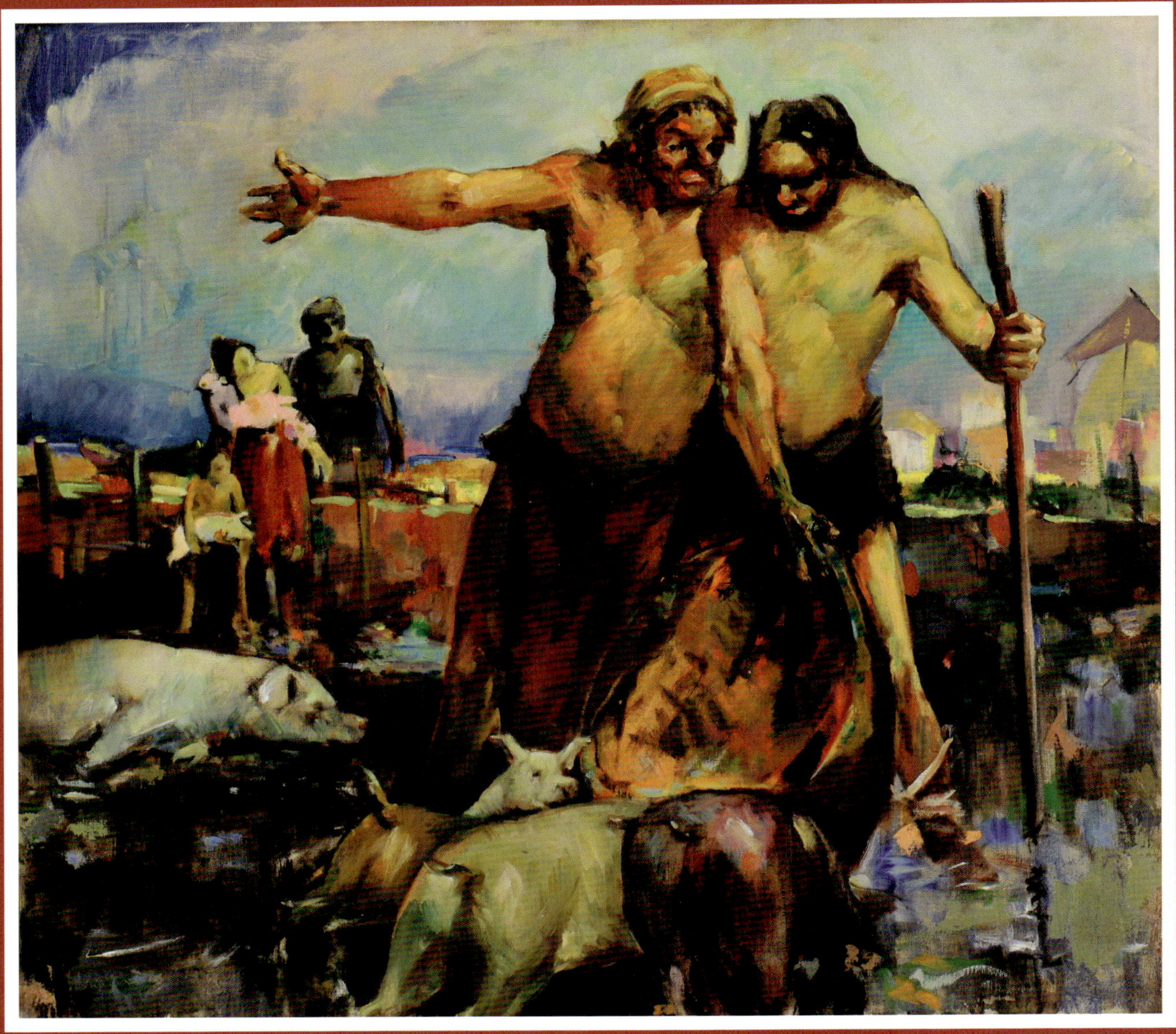

The Prodigal Son, 1927
Oil on canvas, 36 ½ x 40 ¾ inches
Cedar Rapids Museum of Art, Museum purchase. 28.1

THE MAKING OF DAVID McCOSH

Danielle M. Knapp

In 1977, David and Anne McCosh participated in an oral history interview conducted by family friend Phil Gilmore.[1] During the course of the interview the couple reminisced about the earliest years of their careers and the circumstances that had brought them to Eugene, Oregon, in 1934. As the three discussed the challenges of assessing one's own oeuvre, Anne emphatically declared that "a real retrospective will show the first things you ever exhibited." In David's case, these "first things" were oil paintings, watercolors, and lithographs created during his student years at the School of the Art Institute of Chicago (AIC) and as a young struggling artist in the Midwest and New York and at several artist colonies and residencies. This exhibition, *The Making of David McCosh: Early Paintings, Drawings, and Prints*, highlights those years of his life with dual purpose: to thoughtfully examine his body of work from the 1920s and early '30s and to provide those familiar with his celebrated later work a more complete understanding of the entire arc of this extraordinary artist's career.

McCosh's output has always defied traditional categorization within art historical styles. During his life he found strict allegiance to stylistic perimeters to be, at best, distracting and, at worse, repressive, though his own work certainly reflected elements of the artistic communities through which he moved. He was particularly impressed by French painters Paul Cézanne and Henri Matisse, whose work he considered to be honest. An attentive perfectionist, McCosh's immediate concern was always on the task at hand: his visual engagement with his subject and the physical process of his medium.

McCosh's early works—and the sketchbooks and preliminary drawings that accompanied them—illustrate the breadth of his artistic activity between 1923, when he enrolled at the AIC, and 1934, when he relocated permanently to Eugene with wife, Anne Kutka McCosh, to teach at the University of Oregon (while Anne never completely abandoned her creative practice, she did not aggressively pursue her own artistic career after her marriage to David). McCosh's long association with the University of Oregon Department of Art and his contribution to Northwest painting have often eclipsed his multi-faceted beginnings, and perhaps rightfully so. After all, it was only after leaving the Midwest that he progressed beyond the American social regionalism that often heavily tinged much of his earliest work, and it was out west that he reached a critical point in his relationship with his subject matter, favoring direct observation of nature over other influences. In his later years, his work became increasing abstract, although abstraction was never a consciously intended result, but rather a consequence of his methods of observation.

This exhibition draws heavily upon the art and archival materials contained within the David John McCosh Memorial Collection and the permanent collection of the Jordan Schnitzer Museum of Art. We are deeply grateful for select loans of important early works from the Smithsonian American

Danielle Knapp received her BA in art history from Eastern Washington University and her MA in art history and museum studies certificate from the University of Oregon.

Art Museum, the Cedar Rapids Museum of Art, the Cedar Rapids Chamber of Commerce, Wayne State University, and private collectors, which ensured that this survey would be as comprehensive as possible. Most of the works in this exhibition have never before been publicly displayed in Eugene, and the artwork is further supported by primary documents contained in the McCosh Memorial Archive. Personal letters and sketchbooks from this period provide insight into McCosh as an emerging professional artist and give a greater sense of the personality of an especially private and introspective man. His sense of humor and sharp wit, not so obvious in the later paintings he exhibited in Oregon, were often on full display in his earlier, more representational artworks. McCosh's observations, whether in paint, pencil, or ink, recorded his active interest in the quotidian charms of his immediate environment.

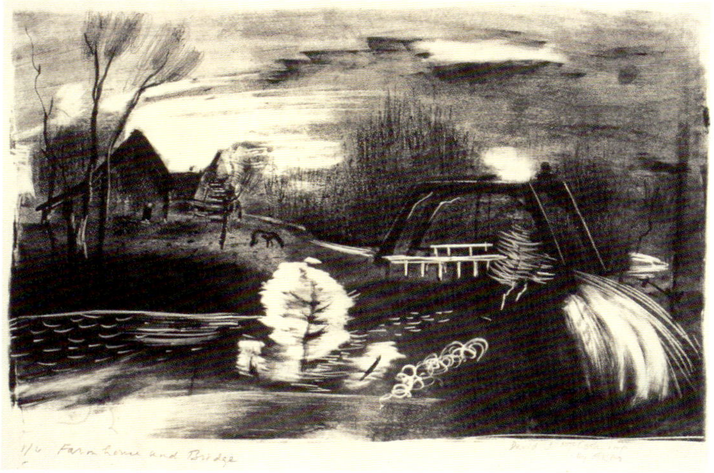

Farm Home and Bridge, c. 1930. Lithograph, 8 x 12 ¼ inches.
Jordan Schnitzer Museum of Art

David John McCosh was born in 1903, at a decisive moment in the American heartland's cultural development. A decade had passed since Chicago hosted the World's Columbian Exhibition, just some two hundred miles from McCosh's birthplace of Cedar Rapids, Iowa. The legacy of this international event remained a critical element of the Chicagoan zeitgeist for a long period to follow. Though the city failed in its bid to replace New York as the cultural and economic center of the country, Chicago saw its global reputation expand beyond its gritty industrial roots. The International Exposition of Modern Art, known more familiarly as the Armory Show, was exhibited at the Art Institute just twenty years later. The 632 paintings, drawings, and sculptures by European avant-garde artists, such as Marcel Duchamp and Pablo Picasso (and even one Chicago native, Manierre Dawson), left a shocked and muttering crowd in its wake. There was already significant backing for abstract art in Chicago—Americans Arthur Wesley Dow and Jerome Blum, among others, had been exhibiting their own decidedly modern artwork locally in the years leading up to the Armory Show—but never before had the community been so blatantly confronted by the dramatic changes happening in contemporary art. The more conservative Beaux Arts–minded students at the AIC, incensed by Henri Matisse's distortion of the female form, even burned in effigy three copies of his paintings and held a mock trial for a figure dubbed "Henry Hair-Mattress."

Despite the distaste expressed by many of Chicago's more vocal residents, the exhibition was extraordinarily well-attended: more than 188,000 visitors, an amount equal to 8 percent of the city's population, saw the Armory Show between March 24 and April 16, 1913. This attendance record surpassed the crowd that had visited the show during its month-long debut run in New York, even though that venue included twice the amount of artwork shown in Chicago. Deemed radical, perverted, or just merely ugly by its critics, the Armory Show ignited community fervor for a greater discussion of the arts and stimulated Chicago's emergence as the thriving cultural hub of which its residents had dreamed since the World's Columbian Exhibition.

These happy circumstances were, however, short-lived: the country entered the First World War in 1917 and suffered the economic depression that followed in 1929. In Charlotte Moser's essay "'In the Highest Efficiency': Art Training at the School of the Art Institute of Chicago," she described the war's profound effect on the city as having "wrenched Chicago as it did the rest of the country into confronting the new social and economic conditions of the twentieth century."[2] Amid great emotional and financial strains, the 1920s saw art in the Midwest, rather than streamline into one distinctive style, branch further into various art movements that frequently reflected contemporary attitudes about personal expression, modernity, national and regional identity, and social change.

As the son of the local cemetery's superintendent and one of four children in the household,[3] David McCosh's early life in Cedar Rapids was by no means upscale, but it was pleasant. He attended Washington High School (from which well-known regionalist painters Grant Wood and Marvin Cone had graduated in 1910), where he was an associate editor and artist for the school's magazine *The Pulse* until receiving his diploma in 1922. McCosh's early interest in newspaper work and cartooning stuck with him through adulthood, and in a 1933 letter to Anne Kutka, he wrote wistfully of his recent meeting with a writer from the *Chicago Tribune*: "He had a lot of good yarns as usual and I wished again as I always do when I go over there (like a kid seeing a fireman) that I had stuck to my original ambition and grown up to be a reporter too."[4] McCosh attended Coe College in Cedar Rapids for one academic year (1922–23) before transferring to the prestigious AIC. At Coe, he had studied under the AIC-educated Cone, but substantial arts education was almost nonexistent. Cone (whose official appointment was actually instructor of French) taught one course in "Free-hand Drawing," the Greek Department hosted a class on Greek and Roman art, and an offering in art appreciation was provided by the Department of Home Economics.[5] McCosh's desire for a competitive arts education necessitated a move to Chicago, where he would find greater opportunities than anywhere else in the region.

The AIC's institutional history dates to 1866, when a group of local artists, inspired by the structure of the art academies of Europe, founded the Chicago Academy of Design. Following years of misfortune (the Chicago Fire of 1871 destroyed the Academy's first permanent residence), financial struggle, and staffing turmoil, the restructured and newly renamed Chicago Academy of Fine Arts was incorporated in 1879 and officially became The Art Institute of Chicago three years later. The occasion of the World's Colombian Exposition of 1892–93 saw opportunity for the institution to receive a much larger permanent space when it took over the two-story lakefront fairground building that had been home to the World's Congress of Religions. By the time McCosh enrolled at the AIC in 1923, the school was well-known for uniquely combining the influences of the European academies' pedagogy with the industrial aesthetic of the graphics and printing businesses prevalent throughout Chicago. Studying under such artists as Frederick Victor Poole, Wellington J. Reynolds, and J. Allen St. John, McCosh fine-tuned his skills in anatomical drawing and composition while also taking classes in the printmaking techniques of intaglio and lithography. A talented colorist, he would begin his paintings with a very limited palette and expertly blend his paints so as to recreate the full range of colors he saw in nature. Norman L. Rice, who entered the program just a few years after McCosh, shared his recollections of the typical course load at the AIC:

> We worked not only in our assigned classrooms but all over the Museum—drawing the casts, the stairways, the decorative arts galleries, and spilling over in to the vast, richly endowed collections of the Field Museum. And of course, there was the busy lakefront and all of Chicago. [...] Our drawing classes were methodical and thorough. We were kept to the hard discipline of cast drawing for our full first year, but we had a good opportunity to draw the figure, too, and plenty of work with color and a chance to do some compositional work as well.[6]

Affiliation with the AIC also ensured that McCosh was exposed to the work of important artists from outside the region. The New York–based Ashcan School painters, who eschewed formal academic styles and traditional subject matter in favor of realistic representations of contemporary urban life, visited the campus in the 1920s. Each year, several exhibitions of important western nineteenth- and twentieth-century artists (George Inness, Odilon Redon, Mary Cassatt, and George Bellows, to name just a few), historical and contemporary Asian art, and the work of current students and alumni were hosted at the AIC. McCosh enjoyed friendships with many of his classmates who would go on to have illustrious careers in Chicago and beyond, among them Ivan Albright, Francis Chapin, Theodore Roszak, and Andrew Vincent, a Kansas-born artist hailing from Oregon.

McCosh graduated from the Department of Drawing, Painting, and Illustration in 1926 with "Class Honorable Mentions in Illustration and Etching." The following year, both he and Chapin entered a rigorous painting competition in which contestants were assigned the subject of "The Prodigal Son," and were required to submit a preliminary sketch of their composition in six hours, followed by a finished painting in under a month's time. Happily, the two friends each won one of the monetary prizes awarded to support foreign travel—McCosh, the John Quincy Adams Scholarship, and Chapin, the Brian Lathrop Scholarship—and they made plans to visit England, France, Ireland, and Italy together for a period of eight months the following year.

In Europe, McCosh and Chapin sketched the architecture of Florence, painted French sailboats at the water's edge in Roscoff, and observed the leisurely crowds of pedestrians on the streets of London. McCosh's *L'Aquarelliste* (cover), a portrait of Chapin, is one of the many vibrant oil paintings that resulted from this trip. Though Chapin's back is turned to the viewer, the composition's unconventional vantage point works especially well as a portrait of the *aquarelliste* ("watercolorist") in action. McCosh skillfully conveyed his friend's height and thin figure by filling the plane with Chapin's long frame, cropping his head at the top of the picture plane and his legs at the bottom. The small blue book visible in the subject's back pocket was likely one of the many sketchbooks he and the artist always kept close at hand and filled with competent and charming records of their travels. In fact, the bustling street scene Chapin is depicted painting here would have most certainly been a view that both men thoroughly explored in their own sketches first. Upon his return from Europe in 1928 (with, as he recounted during his Gilmore interview, only 37 cents left in his pocket), McCosh continued his studies at the AIC on a full scholarship. The following year, *L'Aquarelliste* was included, along with *Pont Marie—Paris* (page 25) and several other oil paintings from his European trip, in a one-man show at the Little Gallery of the American Federation of Arts in Cedar Rapids.

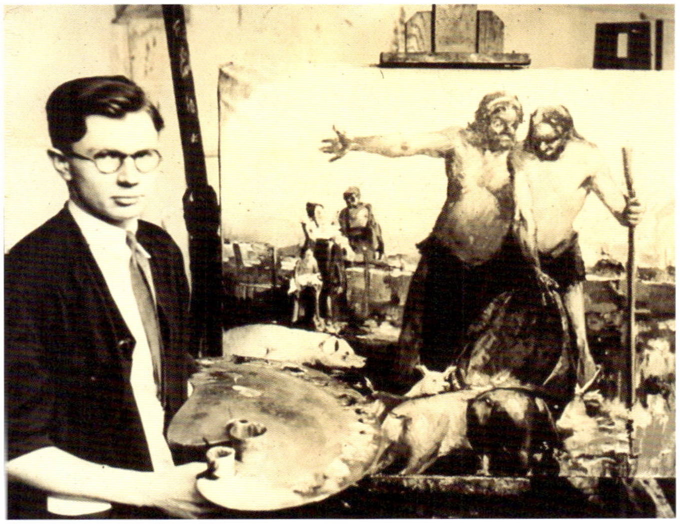

Photo of David McCosh with *The Prodigal Son*, c. 1927.
David John McCosh Memorial Archive. Gift of Anne Kutka McCosh

After finishing his graduate studies, McCosh showed his artwork as frequently as possible, relishing the occasional sale of a painting or a cash prize. He stayed in Chicago for several reasons—in part because of his limited job prospects elsewhere, but equally due to his continued involvement with the AIC and the local art communities. For McCosh, postgraduation life in Chicago meant rooming in boarding houses or apartments shared with friends. His home base was always ready material for his next project, and his watercolors from this period read as spontaneous snapshots of the world around him. Many of these were executed on the spot, but an examination of a larger selection of his work from this period quickly reveals his occasional use of repeated characters and animals in different compositions. McCosh made a habit of mentally gathering certain postures or figural groupings he found interesting into a sort of "visual toolbox."[7] This practice was by no means limited to McCosh, but a comparison of the various instances in which his repeating figures appear is revealing of his developing compositional eye. As an extension of this methodology, McCosh also frequently revisited entire scenes in as many as four different media, delighting in the potentials of paint or ink to reveal something new about his chosen subject.

In summer 1930, McCosh was awarded a Louis Comfort Tiffany Foundation Fellowship and relocated to Oyster Bay, Long Island, for two months. The foundation, which was started by Tiffany in 1918 to promote young artists, afforded its residents the chance to stay at the sprawling sixty-two acre Laurelton Hall estate and devote their time to creating new work and interacting with other artists. It was here that McCosh met another promising young painter on fellowship, Anne Kutka, from Yonkers, New York. The amiable Kutka was an accomplished artist and no doubt made a considerable impression on her new friend: she had studied under drawing instructor Kimon Nicolaides at the Art Students League and was employed as the manager of the Gladys Roosevelt Dick Gallery in New York City. Though brief, their shared time at Oyster Bay became the foundation of a strong relationship, and in the years following, the couple maintained a regular correspondence from their respective home bases of Chicago and New York. They wrote frequently on the subjects of their own artwork, gallery shows they attended, mutual friends in the art community, and the state of contemporary art. When McCosh attended an exhibition of drawings by Matisse in Chicago in the early '30s, he shared his positive reactions with Kutka in a letter: "I liked [Matisse's drawings] because they looked so honest. There is such an epidemic of super smart drawings now that his simple straightforward ones with no tricks were quite a relief. Does everyone in N.Y. try to make tricky effects in their drawings now? Everyone here seems to think that the ultimate idea of art."[8]

While at the Tiffany Foundation, McCosh also became friends with Herbert Ferber Silvers, who would later (after the strategic dropping of his last name to distance himself from his early etchings) gain prominence as an abstract expressionist sculptor. The two men stayed in touch after their summer in Oyster Bay and shared an apartment and studio in New York City during the winter of 1931. Speaking in an interview with Irving Sandler in 1968, Ferber described his association with McCosh in the early 1930s:

> [McCosh] began to increase my knowledge of what art was about because here was a man who had really studied in a good art school and who had been in Europe for a year and was a follower of Cézanne. And he opened my eyes to a great many possibilities in painting and sculpture which I wasn't even aware of. [...] a sort of modernism. [...] But it was through David McCosh and Roszak and people who were studying at the Art Students League, a girl [Anne Kutka] who later became McCosh's wife, that I began to meet artists who introduced me to what was more contemporary than even Cézanne at that time, such artists as De Chirico and so on.[9]

McCosh worked as a studio assistant to master lithographer Grant Arnold during the summer 1931 session of the Maverick Art Colony in Woodstock, New York. Arnold had moved to Woodstock the previous year after completing studies at the Art Students League in New York. His presence at Woodstock, where residents enjoyed a rustic and simple lifestyle in the spirit of the colony's idealistic founder Hervey White, helped elevate lithography as a fine art. For McCosh, who had studied printmaking intensively at the AIC, lithography was a way to experience the world via a different medium, the equivalent of looking at his surroundings with fresh eyes. Both he and Chapin had previously worked with Bolton Brown, one of the founding members of the earlier Byrdcliffe colony at Woodstock, while the esteemed older printmaker was in Chicago in 1930. McCosh's lithographs reflect the same interests featured in his contemporaneous sketchbooks, watercolors, and oil paintings: cityscapes, domestic interiors, rural scenes, and character studies. He was as critical of his lithographic attempts as he was with his paintings, and the added complication of working the large lithography press, which required the careful handling of the limestone printing plate and skilled manipulation of the chemical processes, made successful lithograph printing that much more of a challenge. In works such as *Farm Home and Bridge* (page 10), McCosh balanced positive and negative space in an intimate landscape set with a farmhouse, truss bridge, grazing livestock, and rippled river. Large areas of deep black color are offset by the textured outlines of white trees and roads. His simplistic, playful use of line indicated the natural forms present in the rural countryside.

The self-deprecating nature of McCosh's critiques of his own work is revealing of his strongly held value judgments: Color was of the utmost importance. (Displeased with his hurried attempt to paint a carnival shooting gallery scene in 1933, he compared its palette to the colored illustrations that filled the pages of the popular *Western Stories* pulp magazine[10]). For him, honest representation deserved one's full consideration. McCosh was uninspired by the prevailing modernist aesthetic that emphasized abstraction as a theoretical concept, though the fact that it was garnering such high levels of attention was not lost on him. In another letter to Kutka, he stated, "I wish I could do this semiabstract thing that seems so easy for so many people. I can't at all and never do get even a modern idea. I really don't like these overlapping odds and ends of violins and machinery but it seems to be the thing to do."[11] In response to modernist poet Ezra Pound's 1934 call to "Make it new!" the young McCosh would likely have begged, "Keep it real!"

McCosh's Chicago was a city of energy and constant change. He kept well-informed about the current political and economic events throughout the '30s, following with interest the news stories about gangster John "Jake the Barber" Factor, bank closures throughout the region, and the assassination of Chicago mayor Anton Cermak. His representations of daily life in Chicago operate as poignant social commentaries without the harsh edge of politicizing. In *Jockeys* (page 16), he imbued his human subjects with nuanced personality, the realities of their daily lives implicit in expression and gesture. Ever the observant reporter, in this watercolor painting McCosh dutifully captured the no-nonsense poses of the three gruff horsemen in their element. They are perfectly framed within the doorway of the stable without a sense of fussy posturing that would suggest formal group portraiture.

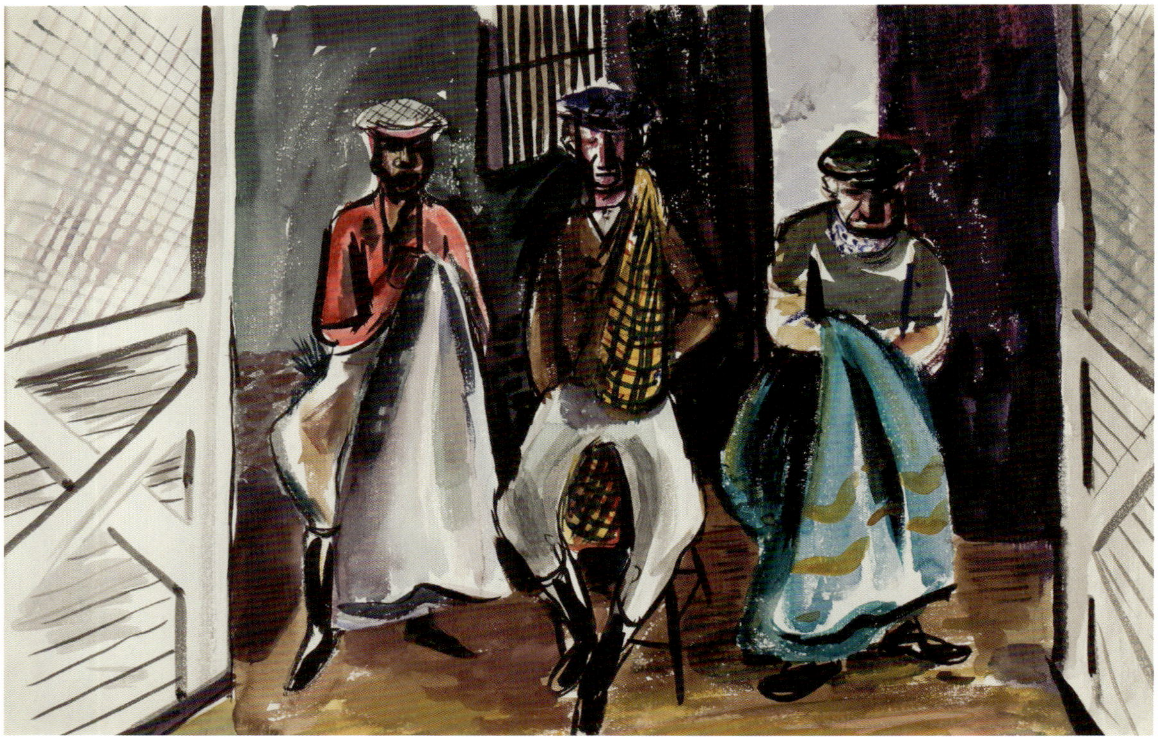

Jockeys, 1934. Watercolor on paper, 15 ⅜ x 22 ½ inches. David John McCosh Memorial Collection

The bright palette in which he worked and his loose rendering of the jockeys' bodies and faces brought an otherwise somber composition to life. McCosh's easy familiarity with the subject matter reveals his frequent attendance at polo matches and horse races, where he filled his sketchbook pages with quick renditions of horses and riders in motion.

A one-man show at the AIC in 1932 included the oil painting *Girl Sewing*, a full-body portrait of a young woman, legs tucked beneath her, thoughtfully contemplating her needle and thread. C. J. Bulliet, the art critic for the *Chicago Evening Post*, was positive in his review of McCosh's exhibition, projecting that ". . . The McCosh room will be popular with summer visitors," and calling McCosh's work "atmospheric" and "sentimental [in the tradition of Midwest cultural figure] Whitcomb Riley."[12] McCosh's career was certainly on an upswing; he began teaching lithography courses at the AIC during the school year and also served as the director and an instructor at the Davenport Municipal Art Gallery (now the Figge Museum of Art) in Davenport, Iowa. He received a commission from the congregation of the Syrian Greek Orthodox Church in Cedar Rapids to paint twenty religious works for the church's sanctuary, a task that caused him a certain amount of consternation. The subject matter was well outside his usual preferences, and for a painter who put such emphasis on direct observation, the job of depicting the various Christian saints according to his patron's specifications was particularly taxing.

A more appropriate venue for his talents arose the following summer when American regionalist painter Grant Wood decided to take action on his long-held vision of providing Midwesterners a local option for an artists' residency. At the time, he was already a household name due to recent paintings such as *American Gothic* and *Stone City*. The small rural town of Stone City, only four miles from Wood's childhood home of Anamosa, had been founded by limestone quarry workers in 1850. The town enjoyed short-lived prosperity in the years before the manufacture of Portland cement in nearby Waterloo bankrupted the quarries' business, leaving the unincorporated town without viable industry and quickly thereafter, without many residents. Since Wood knew the owner of the property, he and fellow painter Adrian Dornbush were granted permission to lease a ten-acre tract of the land and several of the local abandoned buildings.

McCosh's invitation to teach at the inaugural Stone City art colony came directly from Wood. Despite their age difference of twelve years, the two men were well-acquainted from their shared time in Cedar Rapids, having frequently met for painting trips and for friendly meals of steak and "3.2 brew" beer. McCosh's initial reaction to Wood's plan wavered between enthusiasm and skepticism. He had previously been to Stone City, which he later likened to a ghost town,[13] when Wood was amassing preparatory drawings for his titular painting. In the spring, McCosh wrote to Kutka, "The country around [Stone City] is very interesting so should provide all kinds of materials. The idea of the school is to promote a definite direction for painters in the middle west, and, they hope, be the foundation of a new school of painting. I think it's a grand idea in the abstract but whether they will be able to put it across without cranking out a bunch of imitations remains to be seen."[14] In late June 1932, McCosh joined Wood and fellow instructors Francis Chapin, Marvin Cone, Adrian Dornbush, Florence Sprague, and Edward Rowan at the site. Though less than 100 students attended courses during the colony's six-week run, Wood and other faculty members considered their experiment successful and looked forward to the opportunity to bring in additional artists the following year.

McCosh returned to Stone City for its second summer in 1933, which saw a much larger group of students enroll than had for the first session. By this point, his early suspicions about the value of the colony for serious artists had been confirmed, as students misguidedly copied Wood's style rather than internalizing the principles of good art-making to apply in their own work. McCosh noted, however, that the students weren't to be blamed entirely, as "every one [was] forced to paint

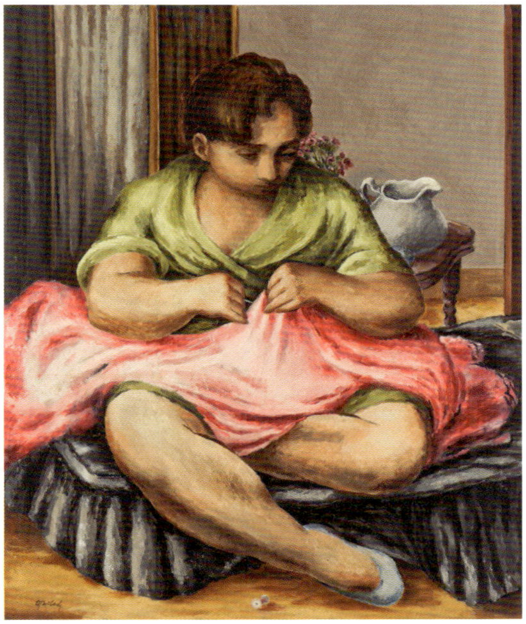

Girl Sewing, 1931. Oil on canvas, 30 x 25 inches.
On loan from Wayne State University Art Collection

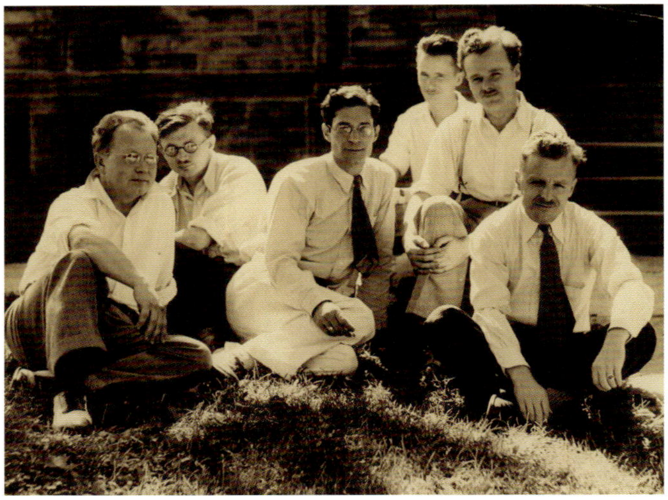

L to R: Wood, McCosh, Rowan, Pyle, Dornbush, and Cone, faculty at Stone City, ca. 1933.
John Barry Jr., photographer. Edward Beatty Rowan papers, Archives of American Art, Smithsonian Institution. (c) Cedar Rapids Museum of Art. Courtesy of Shearon Elderkin.

by Grant's rules."[15] McCosh found the resulting student output, which was exhibited for the public on the weekends, to be rather monotonous. He was humored by Wood's obsession with fostering a new, purely American school of art, intimating in a letter to Kutka that "The big word this year is 'indigenous' and is worked to death. Grant is of course the instigator of all that sort of business and he and Adrian [Dornbush] imagine themselves as Midwestern St. Georges attacking the dragon of French Art. Personally I think they get a little silly sometimes."[16] Despite his misgivings about the expectations imposed on colony students, McCosh remained at his post through the end of the summer. The 1933 session turned out to be the last for the Stone City artists, as financial difficulties brought Wood's colony dreams to an end. McCosh returned to Chicago and taught courses in lithography at the AIC for twelve weeks during the 1933–34 academic year.

In the midst of the Great Depression, in 1933 President Franklin Delano Roosevelt instituted the Civilian Conservation Corps (CCC) as one of several public work relief programs under his New Deal legislation. The CCC was remarkably popular, and in the nine-year period it provided jobs for unskilled laborers, three million American men received paychecks for natural resource conservation projects in rural areas. Employed under the Public Works of Art Project in the spring of 1934, McCosh spent a month at the Camp Chicago Lemont in Willow Springs, Illinois, with the assignment of documenting the CCC workers' activities. The forestry workers, clad in blue coveralls and caps, provided him with an endlessly revolving selection of new subject matter to sketch and paint. McCosh's laboring subjects occupy the subtle gap between anonymous solidarity and individualized character, their efforts commemorated in paintings and drawings of their work and leisure time at the camp.

In fall 1934, Chapin returned from extended travels to Mexico and Duluth and resumed teaching the classes that had been previously assigned to him at the AIC. McCosh had overseen those classes in his absence and with Chapin back at the post he saw his workload significantly diminished. Newly married to Kutka during a trip to Santa Fe, New Mexico, McCosh began to look for a more stable job that would provide him with regular paychecks and new challenges. McCosh's former AIC classmate Andrew Vincent, who had already been teaching at the University of Oregon for five years, sent his friend a letter with the good news that a job opening was immediately available in the Department of Art. "It would be grand to have you out here to work with," ended Vincent's message, "and I'm sure you would enjoy a short stay at least."[17] Fortunately for art students who attended the UO between 1934 and 1970, McCosh's stay in Eugene was far longer than either he or Vincent could have possibly foreseen.

Though this exhibition coincides with the thirtieth anniversary of his passing at age seventy-eight in 1981, McCosh's is a living history, as evidenced by the many contemporary artists (most notably, Craig Cheshire, Mark Clarke, Margaret Coe, Jon Jay Cruson, Harry Widman, and the late Nelson Sandgren) who fondly recall his influence on their own educations. And, despite McCosh's Midwestern beginnings, he is closely cherished as one of Oregon's own. His earliest work is timeless in both subject matter and execution and privileged the artist's observations of real people and places over trends, imagination, or emotion, which foreshadowed the important developments that occurred in his later paintings in Oregon. It is perhaps for this very reason that it offers such a compelling sense of intimacy to all who view it, from those who knew him personally to those who may be experiencing his artwork for the first time now. In the brief essays that follow, McCosh's respective relationships with each of the media in which he worked have been thoughtfully examined by individuals that represent the broad range of viewership who appreciate his artwork—community members, artists, collectors, curators, students, and art historians—underscoring his valuable place in the discussion of twentieth-century American art.

1. Philip Gilmore's wife, Dorothy Gilmore, attended the University of Oregon and was a student of David McCosh in the 1940s. This interview took place over two sessions, on September 27 and October 6, 1977, and its recordings were provided to the Jordan Schnitzer Museum of Art by Dorothy Gilmore in 2002.
2. Sue Ann Prince, *The Old Guard and the Avant-Garde: Modernism in Chicago 1910–1940* (Chicago: University of Chicago Press, 1990), 194.
3. Sadly, John and Anna McCosh's firstborn son died as an infant in 1896.
4. Letter from David McCosh to Anne Kutka, 1933, UO Foundation McCosh Memorial Endowment Archive.
5. Coe College 1922–23 course listing provided by Sara Pitcher, Stewart Memorial Library Archives Assistant, e-mail to author, September 10, 2010.
6. Roger Gilmore, ed. *Over a Century: A History of the School of the Art Institute of Chicago, 1866–1981* (Chicago: The School of the Art Institute of Chicago, 1982), 12–13.
7. The idea of a "visual toolbox" stems from discussions with McCosh Advisory Committee member Roger Saydack and McCosh's former students Craig Cheshire and Mark Clarke.
8. Letter from David McCosh to Anne Kutka, February 1932, McCosh Memorial Endowment Archive.
9. Oral history interview with Herbert Ferber, April 22, 1967–January 6, 1969, Archives of American Art, Smithsonian Institution, www.aaa.si.edu/collections/interviews/oral-history-interview-herbert-ferber-12772, accessed February 18, 2011.
10. Letter from David McCosh to Anne Kutka, January 1933, UO Foundation McCosh Memorial Endowment Archive.
11. Letter from David McCosh to Anne Kutka, December 21, 1933, UO Foundation McCosh Memorial Endowment Archive.
12. C. J. Bulliet, "Institute Galleries to Bristle this Summer," *Chicago Evening Post*, July 19, 1932.
13. Interview with Gilmore, 1977, UO Foundation McCosh Memorial Endowment Archive.
14. Letter from David McCosh to Anne Kutka, April 1932, UO Foundation McCosh Memorial Endowment Archive.
15. Letter from David McCosh to Anne Kutka, 1933, UO Foundation McCosh Memorial Endowment Archive.
16. Letter from David McCosh to Anne Kutka, 1933, UO Foundation McCosh Memorial Endowment Archive.
17. Letter from Andrew Vincent to David McCosh, October 18, 1934, UO Foundation McCosh Memorial Endowment Archive.

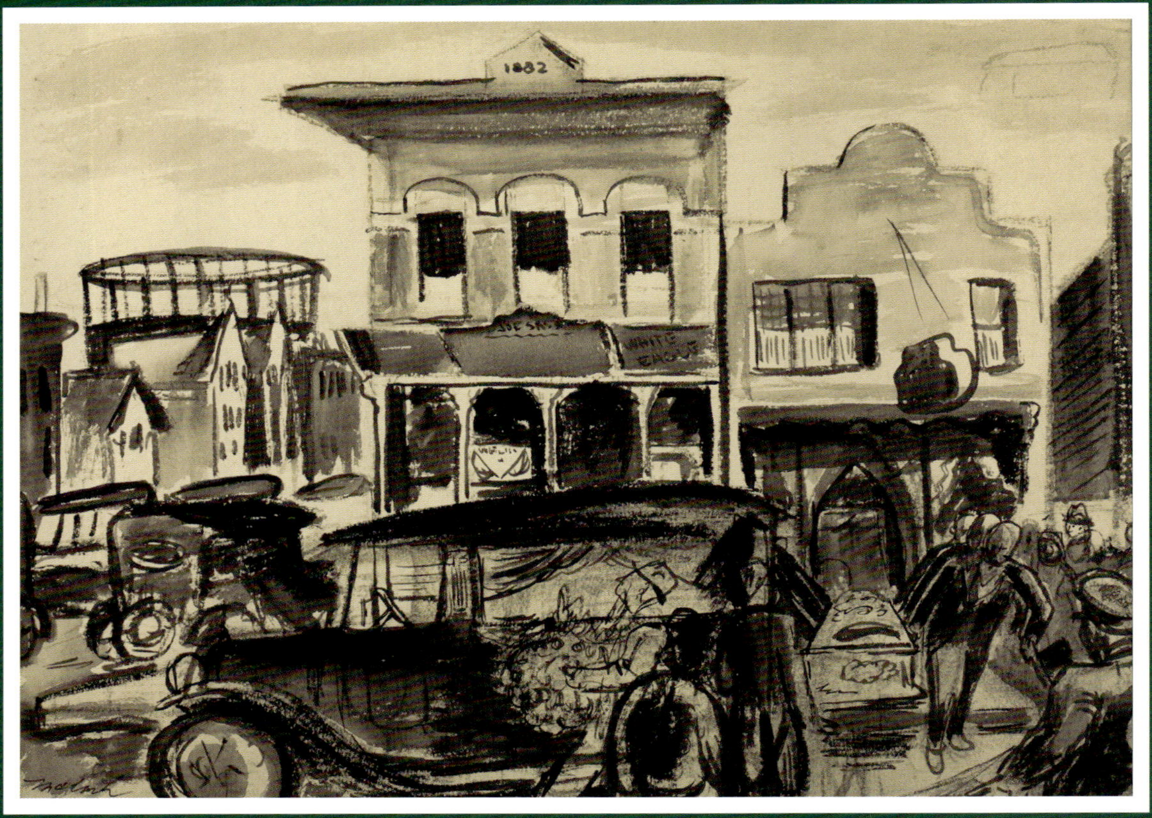

Gangster's Funeral, c. 1930
Ink on paper, 14 x 18 7/8 inches
David John McCosh Memorial Collection

THE EARLY OIL PAINTINGS

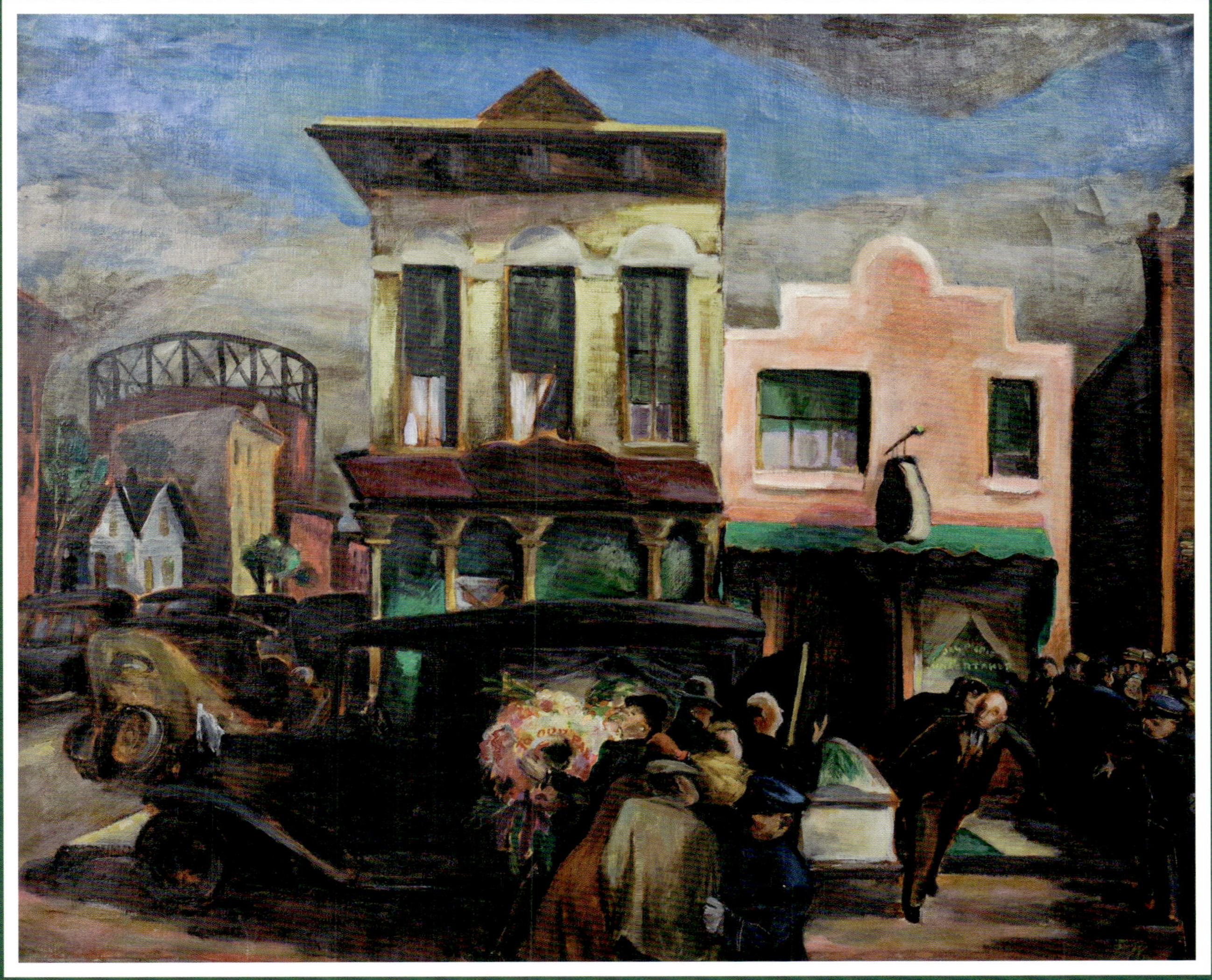

Gangster's Funeral, c. 1930
Oil on canvas, 25 x 30 inches
Jordan Schnitzer Museum of Art

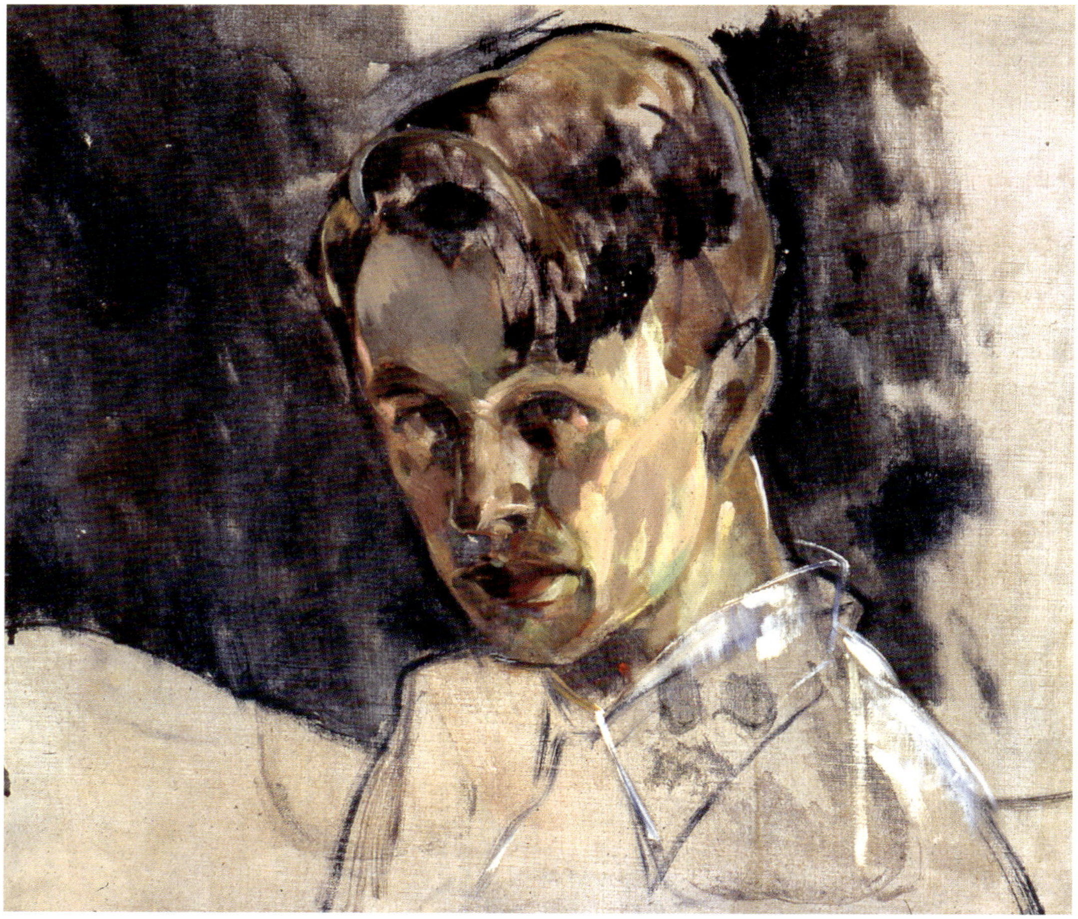

Self-Portrait (Unfinished), 1928
Oil on canvas, 18 x 20 inches
David John McCosh Memorial Collection

THE EARLY OIL PAINTINGS

Margaret Coe

"How you begin a painting depends on what kind of painting you are making," David McCosh stated to an inquiring graduate student at the University of Oregon in the 1970s. Not elaborating on this statement gave a gravitas to this workaday question.

McCosh began his early paintings with traditional umbers and siennas thinned with turpentine and without white. The strong design of *Gangster's Funeral* (page 21) was established in the first layer of paint. He created a single dark mass that undulates across the frontal plane within which the full narrative content is contained. Cars and crowds are nearly lost within it. A figure here, a casket there emerged in a second, thicker layer of paint and rhythmically divided the oppressive darkness. The lightest light is a wreath inscribed with the words "our pal," and it's being plunged into ultimate darkness.

One of David McCosh's fundamental tenets in his teaching was the equality in importance of negative space. The backgrounds in the figurative paintings *The Foreman* (page 24), *Girl Sewing* (page 17), and *The Flagman* (page 27) are relevant and fully integrated in the whole color design. Stylistically, the early figurative paintings may bring to mind the realism movements of the 1930s: Midwest regionalism, urban realism, or the social realism of the WPA muralists. But the intent, mood, and coloration are McCosh's own. These are beautifully composed images of individuals in their work or domestic environments—alone.

It's been suggested that Europeans understood Americans only after seeing the Edward Hopper show that toured the continent in 2002. There's a sense of isolation in early McCosh paintings as well. A windmill catches the breeze in *The White Mill* (page 28). It arises from the stillness of outbuildings in the warm foreground plane to join the dark, cool landscape of the background. This work was painted with the sophistication of Paul Cézanne, whose work had a profound influence on the young McCosh. Continuous observation of color relationship in nature and on the canvas was a legacy from Cézanne that McCosh passed on to his students.

A remarkably successful sabbatical leave of 1949–50 (to Cohasset Beach, Washington; San Miguel de Allende, Mexico; and New Mexico) marked the introduction to McCosh's signature late style. His newer work was abstract, but was still grounded in the act of seeing. Upon first seeing these developments, Anne Kutka McCosh had enthusiastically exclaimed, "You've got it now, boy!" In McCosh's improvisational style of painting, beginning was a perpetual state. Drawing was more likely to be the final action than the first. The language was one of immediacy, of finding an equivalent in paint of a particular experience, and this is the language he spoke in Mexico, New Mexico, and the deep woods of Oregon.

Margaret Coe (BS, 1963; MFA, 1978) is a Eugene-based painter who studied under David McCosh at the University of Oregon. She is a former adjunct assistant professor at the University of Oregon and instructor at Lane Community College, and her work has been exhibited widely.

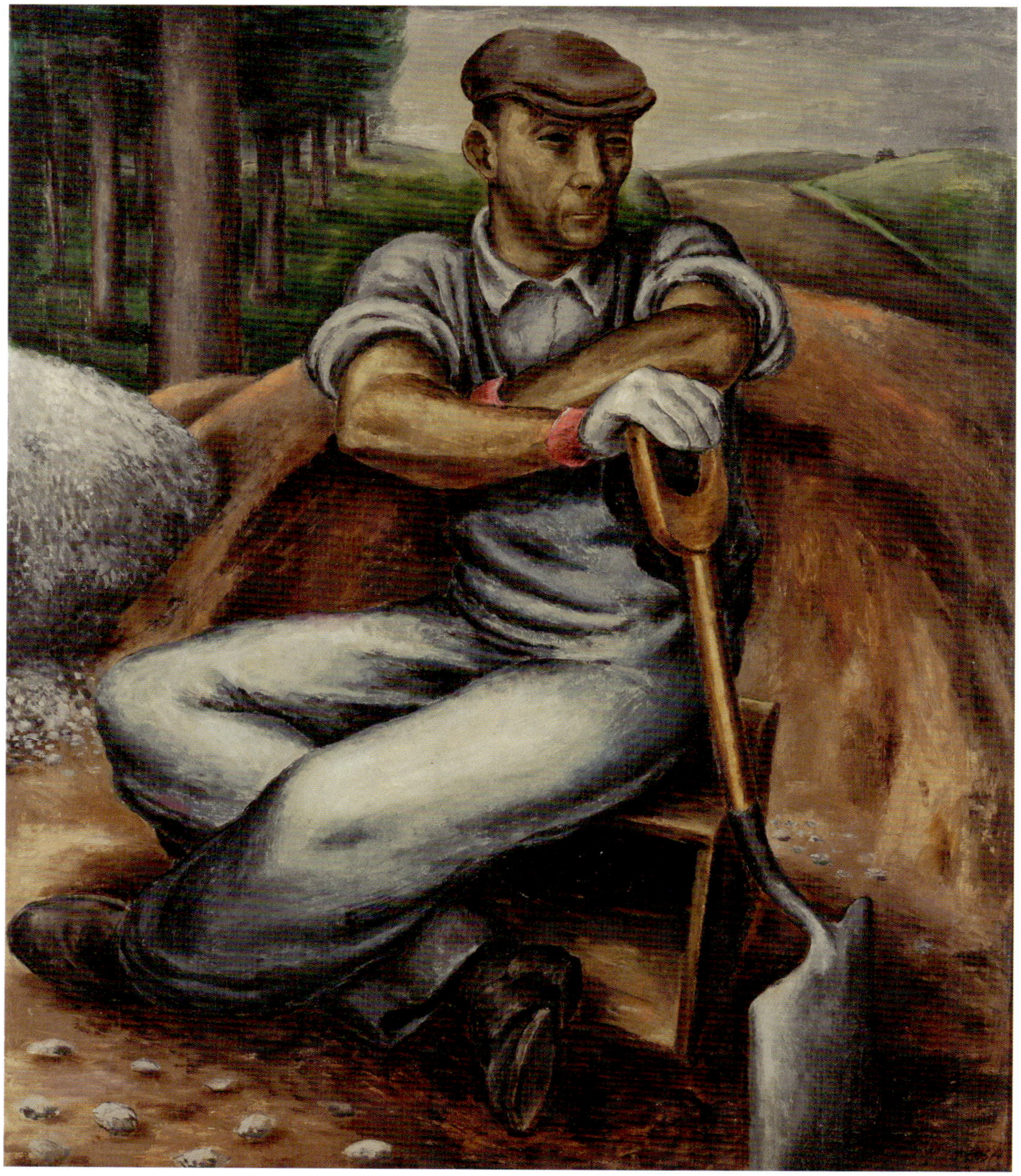

The Foreman, 1932
Oil on canvas, 30 ¼ x 20 inches
On loan from Wayne State University Art Collection

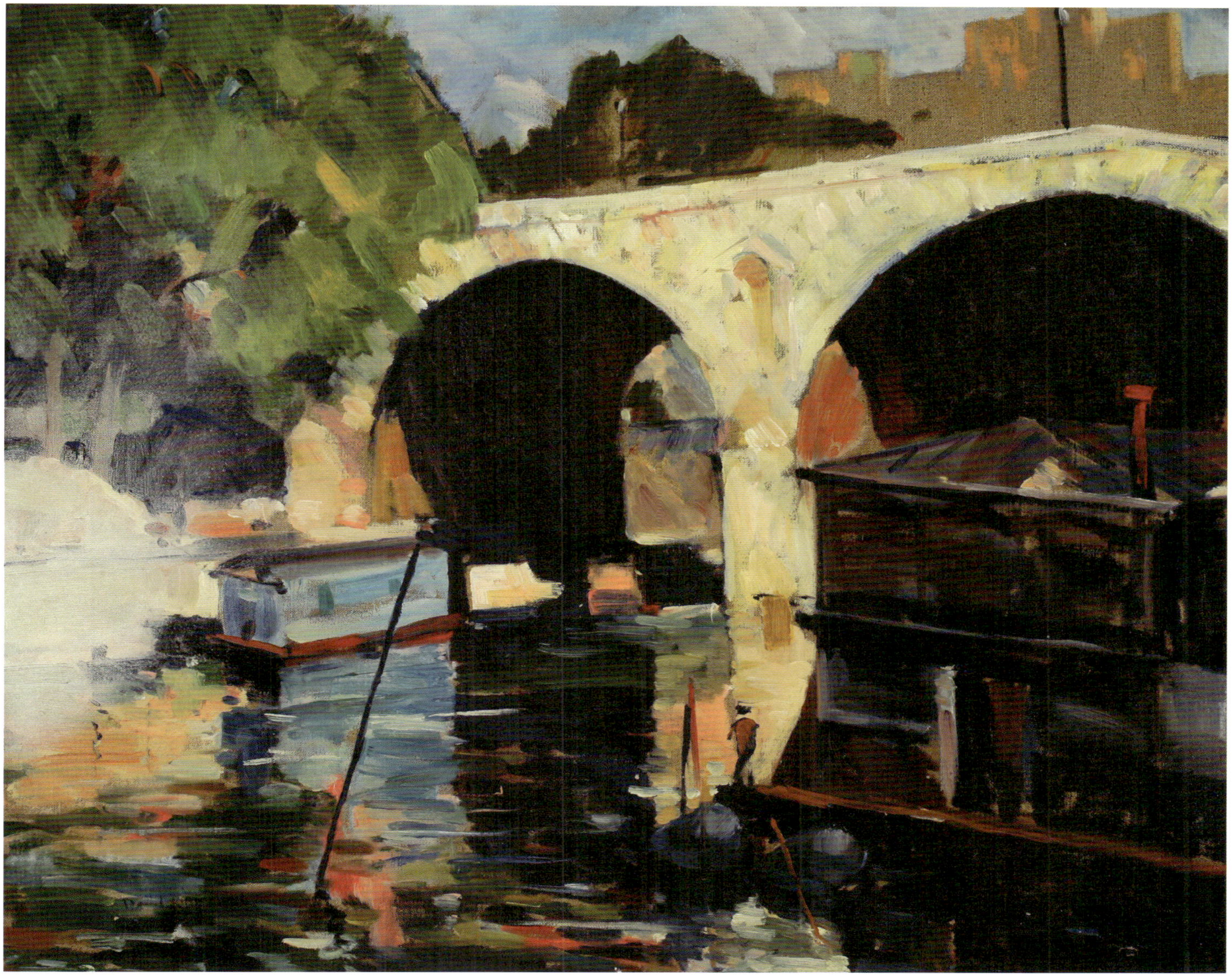

Pont Marie — Paris, c. 1930
Oil on canvas, 19 ⅛ x 24 inches
Cedar Rapids Museum of Art
On loan from the Cedar Rapids Chamber of Commerce.
L1983.15.6

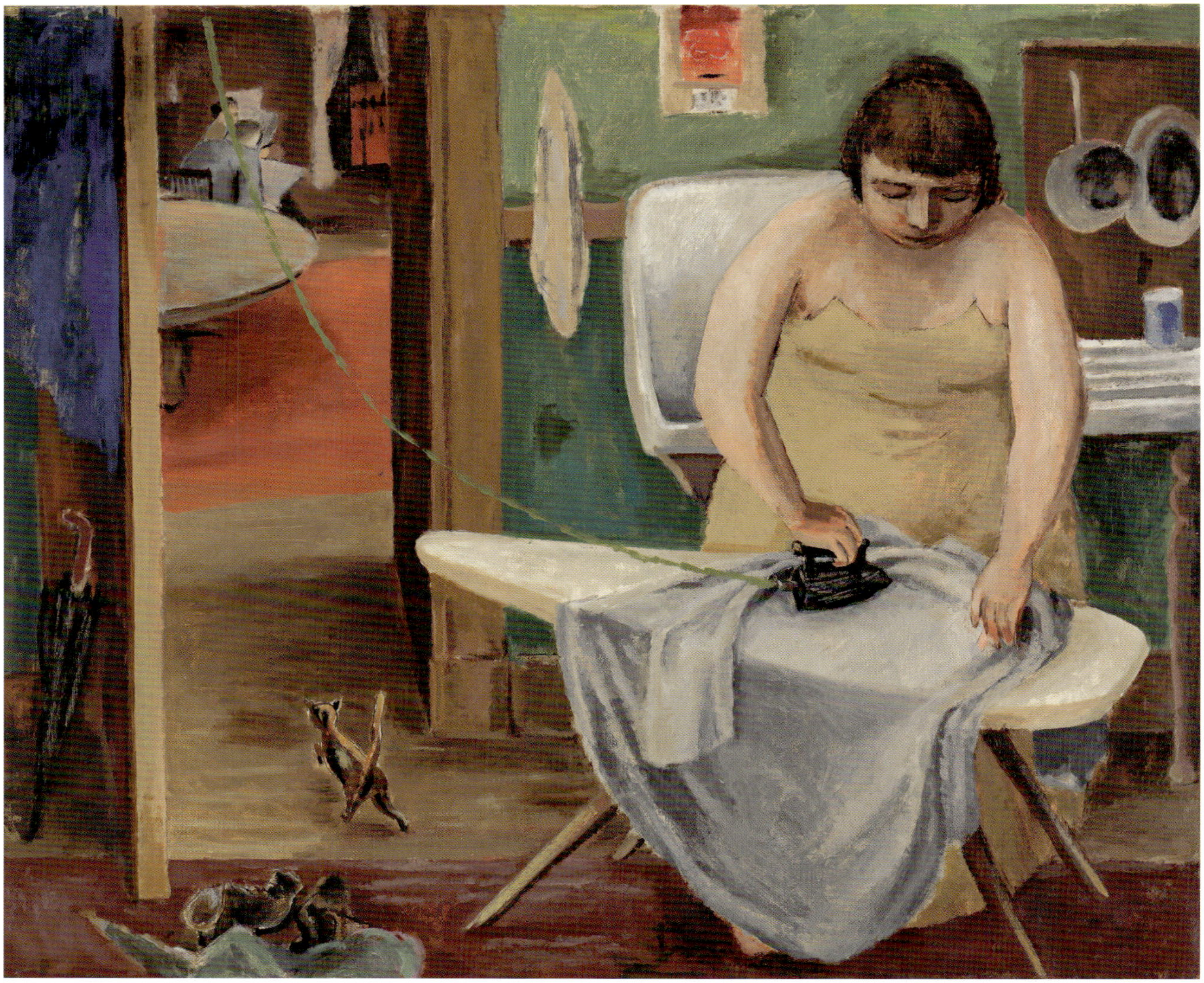

Woman Ironing, 1931
Oil on canvas, 25 x 30 inches
On loan from Smithsonian American Art Museum
Gift of Mrs. Anne Kutka McCosh

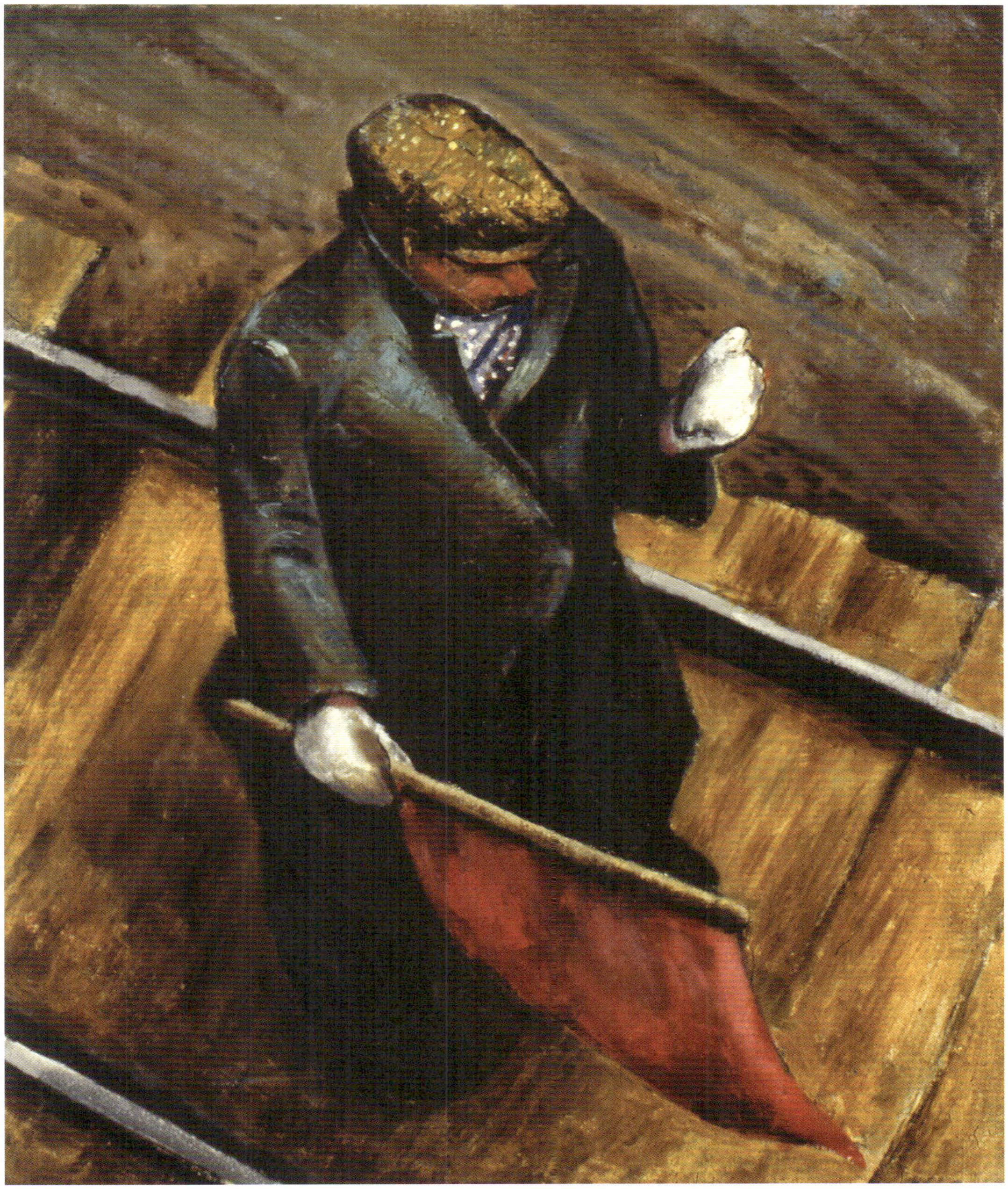

The Flagman, c.1931–32
Oil on linen, 24 x 20 inches
David John McCosh Memorial Collection

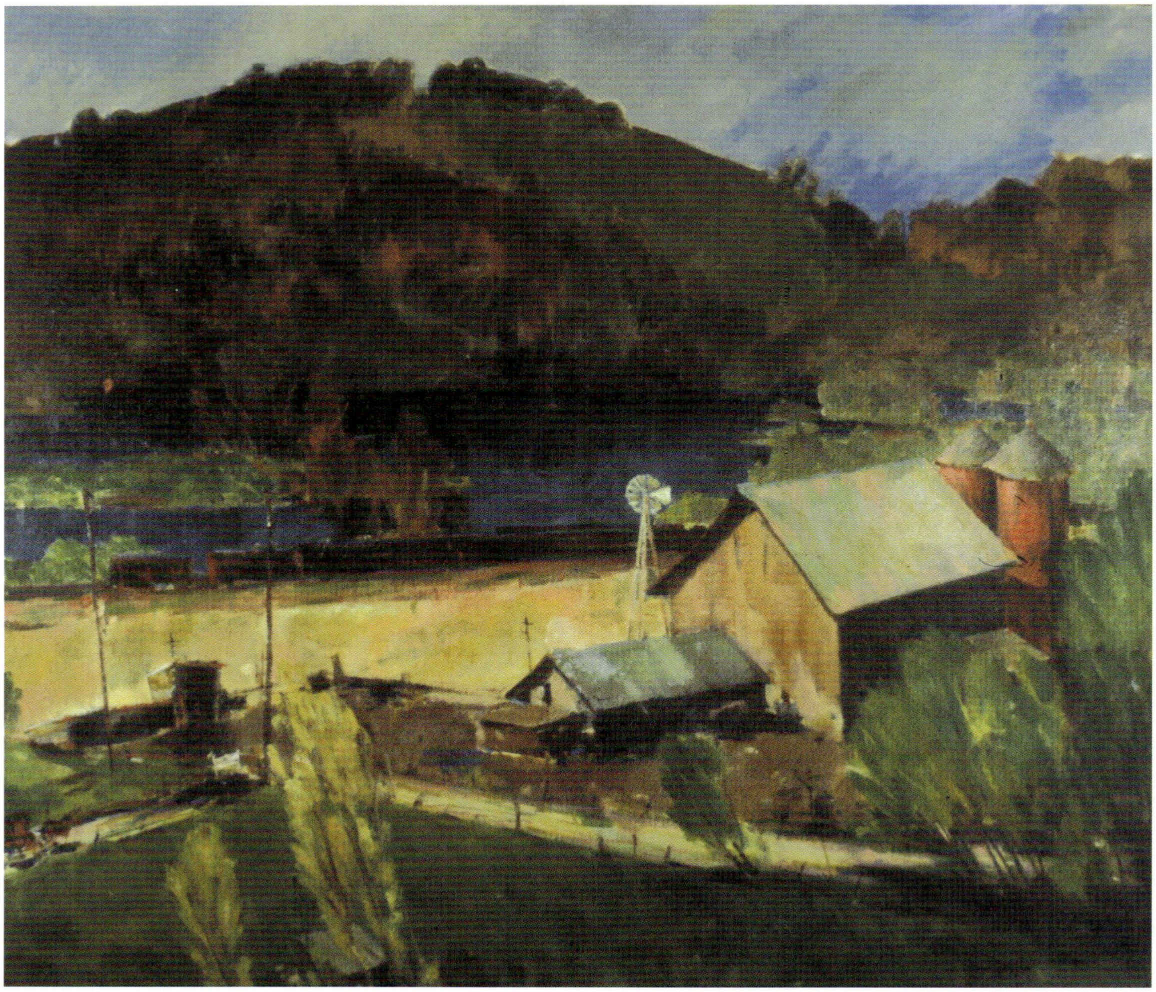

The White Mill, 1929
Oil on canvas, 30 x 40 inches
Jordan Schnitzer Museum of Art

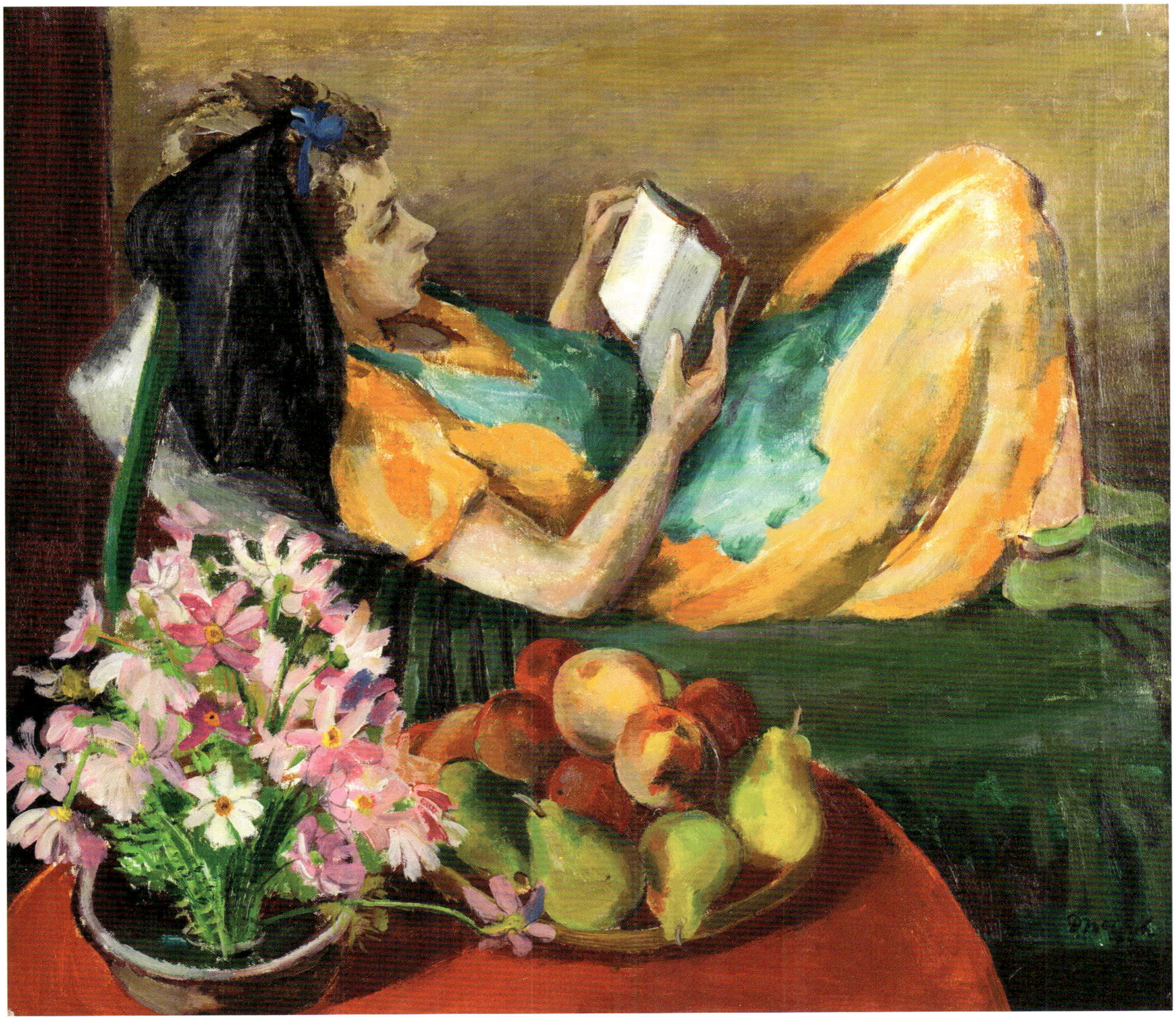

Concentration (Portrait of Anne McCosh), 1934
Oil on canvas, 18 x 20 inches
David John McCosh Memorial Collection

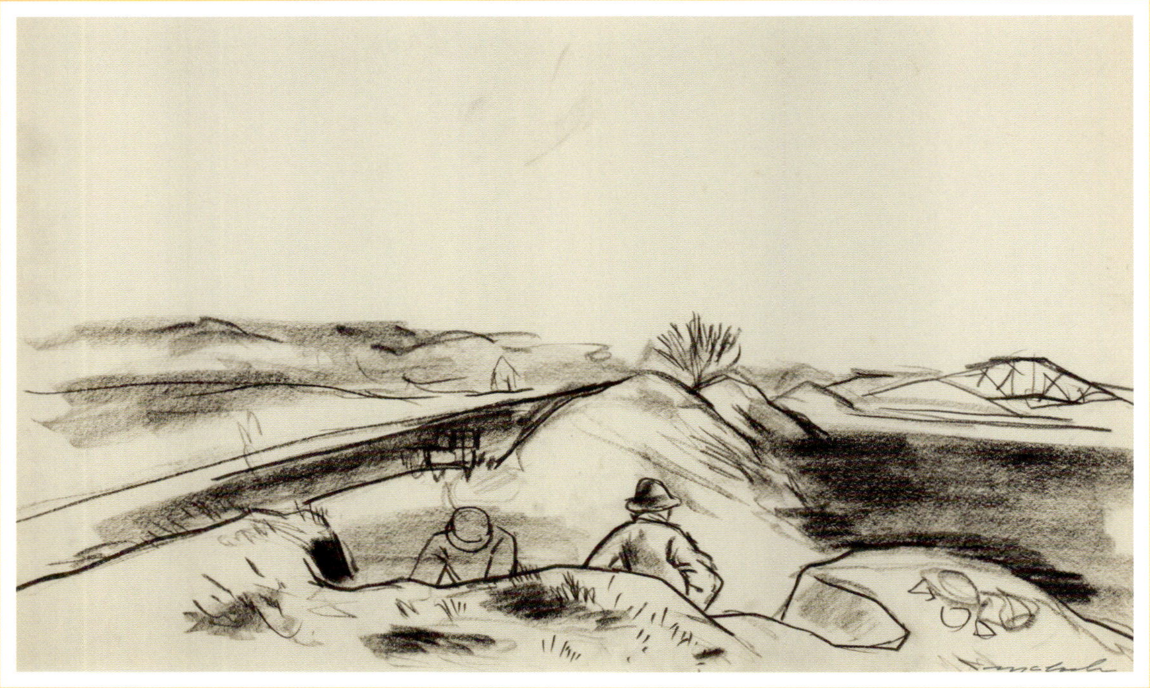

The Reservoir, 1934
Charcoal on paper, 12 ¼ x 18 ¾ inches
David John McCosh Memorial Collection

THE EARLY WATERCOLORS

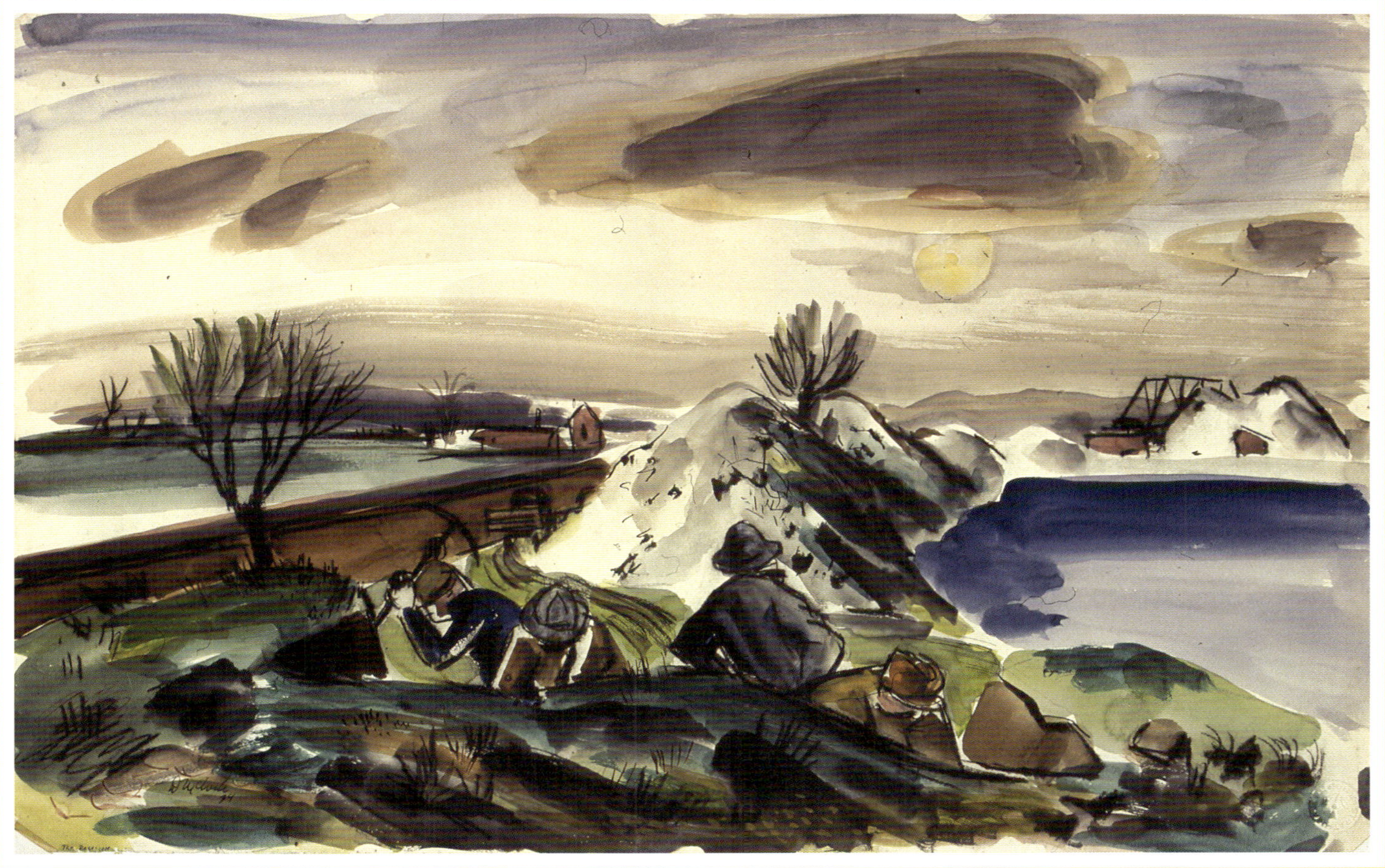

The Reservoir, 1934
Watercolor, ink, and charcoal on paper, 14½ x 23 inches
Jordan Schnitzer Museum of Art

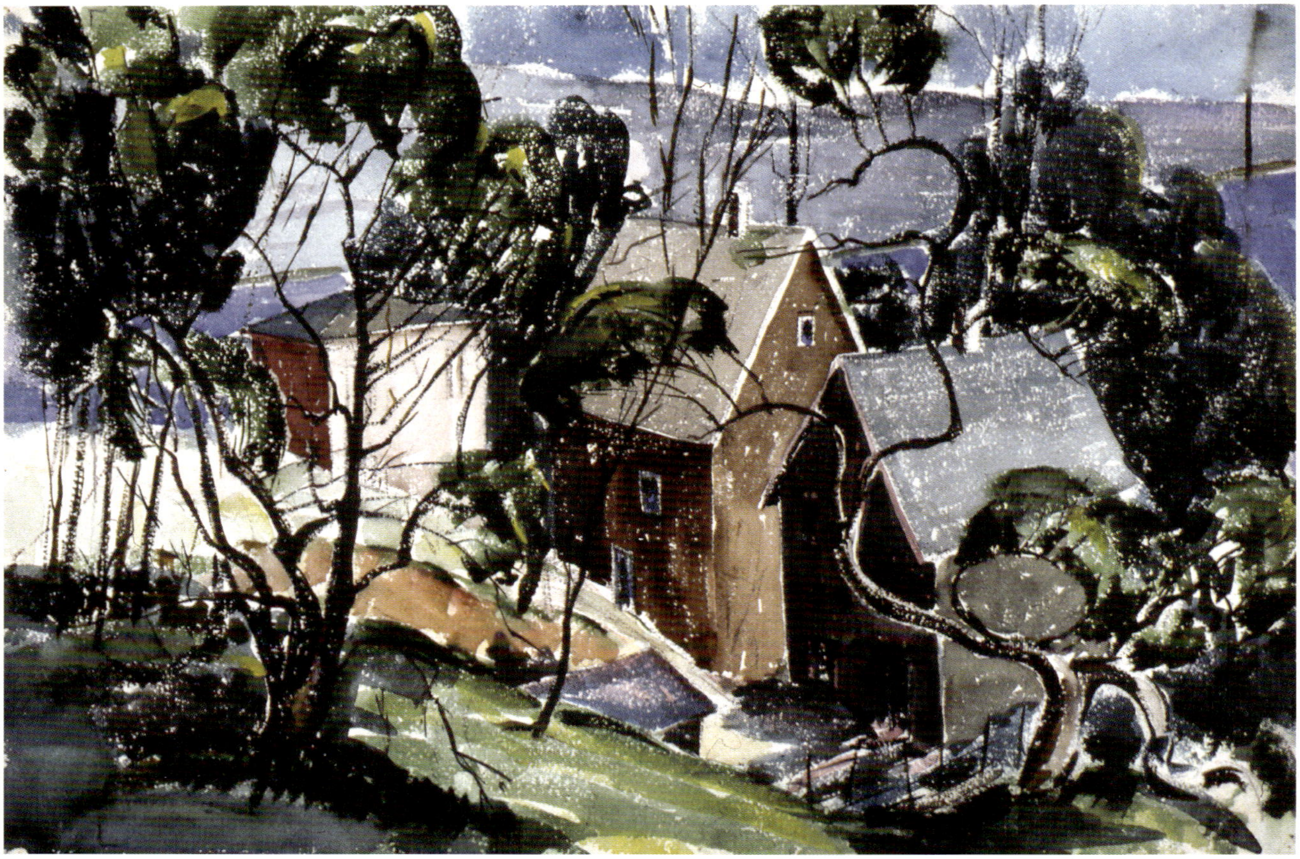

Oyster Bay, 1930
Watercolor on paper, 15 ½ x 22 ⅜ inches
David John McCosh Memorial Collection

THE EARLY WATERCOLORS

Aleksandra Globig and June Irene Koehler

David McCosh's watercolor *Lake Lucerne, Switzerland* (page 34), which dates to his 1927–28 trip to Europe, presents the familiar tropes of early twentieth-century landscape paintings, as demonstrated by the idyllic Swiss vista, punctuated by the twin spires of a gleaming white chapel. This structure, along with the other architectural features in the painting, is meticulously rendered, while the body of water in the midground and the suggestion of land in the foreground anchor the composition. The bold strokes of yellow and orange in the top half of the work serve to further differentiate the man-made from the natural.

In contrast to the pigment-rich *Lake Lucerne* with its thick application of paint, *Reflections, France* (page 35) presents a more subdued scene with its softer color palette. The faint blue-gray wash applied to the entire sheet offers a sense of tranquility to the port, which is bathed in morning light. The water-saturated tones in the sky and sea are similar enough that the two seem to bleed into one another. Though the buildings and boats are rendered with bolder colors and more detail, their velvety, rippling reflections demand as much attention from the viewer as the physical entities that they mirror.

In contrast to these European works, where a distinctly touristic gaze may be noted, McCosh's post-Europe trip watercolors attempt to momentarily freeze the fleeting happenings of everyday life. Bracing himself with his left arm and straining to reach the upper corner of the window with a visibly soaked cloth, the figure in *Window Washer* (page 36) is caught in the middle of his chore. Coupled with the towering exterior of a projecting bay window, the plant forms and abstract interior views glimpsed through the window add to the dominating impression of verticality. The subtle suggestions of specific architectural details are seen in the loosely rendered brick and ironwork. Deep emerald greens, ruby reds, sapphire blues, and other jewel tones give the scene a rich, yet playful, quality. This watercolor of 1929 characterizes McCosh's desire to capture the ephemeral moments of city life.

McCosh's interest in daily life extended from the individual to the crowd, as seen in *State Street Crossing* (page 36), which presents a far more chaotic atmosphere than *Window Washer*. The presence of the trolley, stately architectural details, and throngs of commuters clothed in sophisticated business attire accurately convey the congestion of one of Chicago's busiest streets. Though most of the figures are merely suggested, those in the immediate foreground are hardly anonymous. Their facial features are highly articulated, as are the forms of their bodies, which project a monumental presence.

In later works, McCosh's attention to figuration is married to his interest in landscape. While there are figures present in many of his early landscapes and cityscapes, his watercolors from this period seek to capture the overall atmosphere of a setting rather than the particularities of certain individuals. In contrast, the figures that populate his later watercolors, such as *Lakeshore Swimmers in December* (page 39), are endowed with more identifiable personalities, and as such, represent his evolving artistic vision.

Aleksandra Globig and June Irene Koehler are graduate students in the Department of Art History at the University of Oregon and curatorial interns at the Jordan Schnitzer Museum of Art.

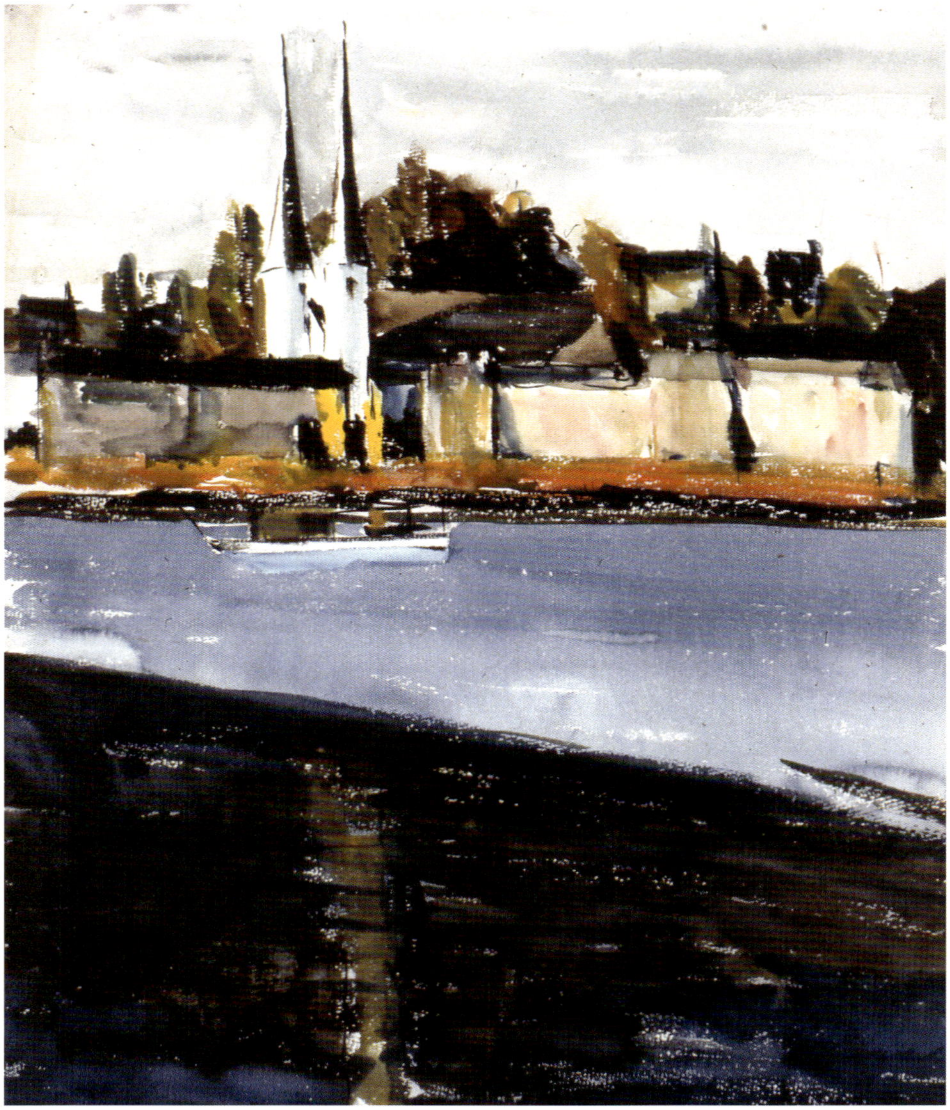

Lake Lucerne, Switzerland, 1928
Watercolor on paper, 15 ½ x 22 ⅜ inches
David John McCosh Memorial Collection

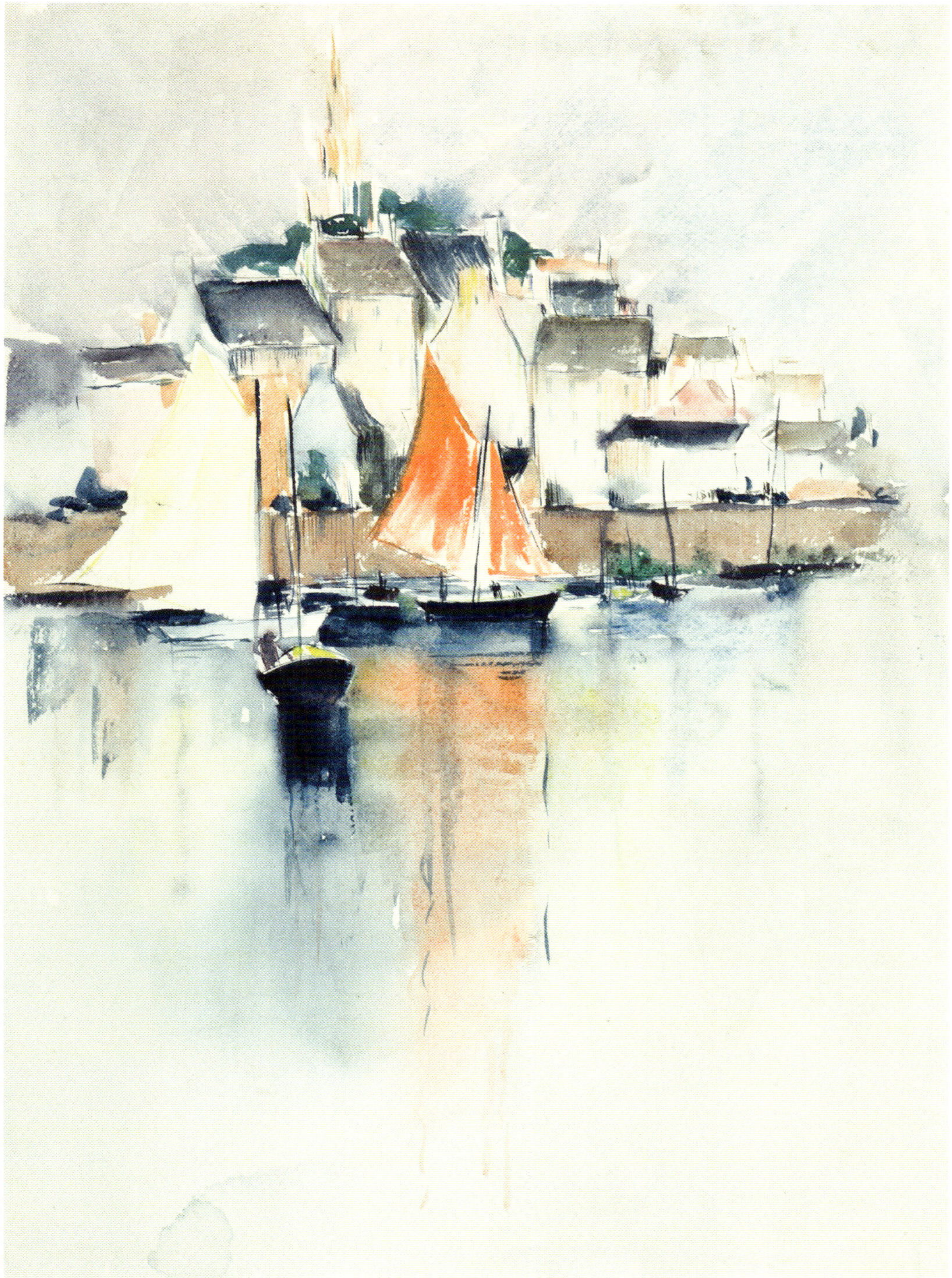

Reflections, France, c. 1930
Watercolor on paper, 14 ¾ x 11 inches
Jordan Schnitzer Museum of Art

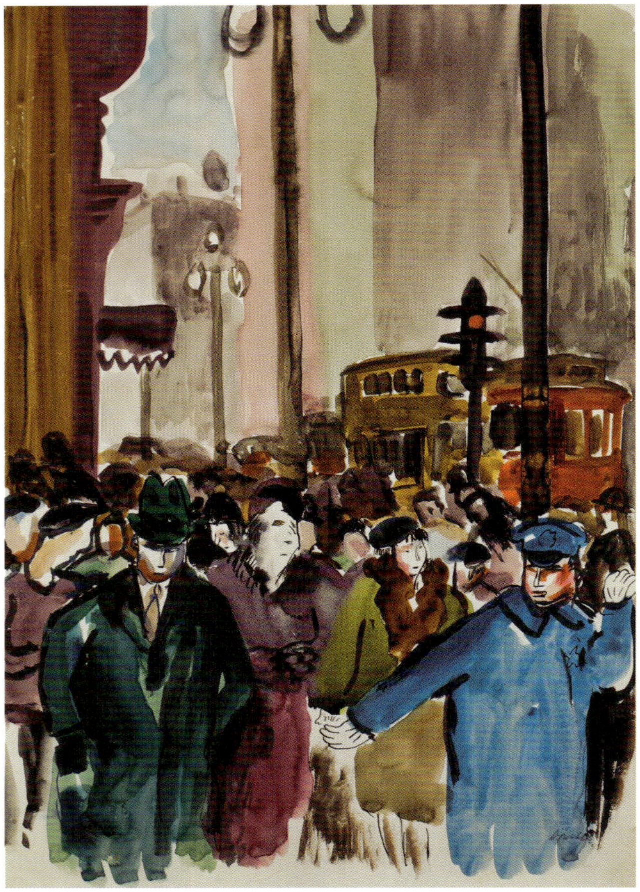

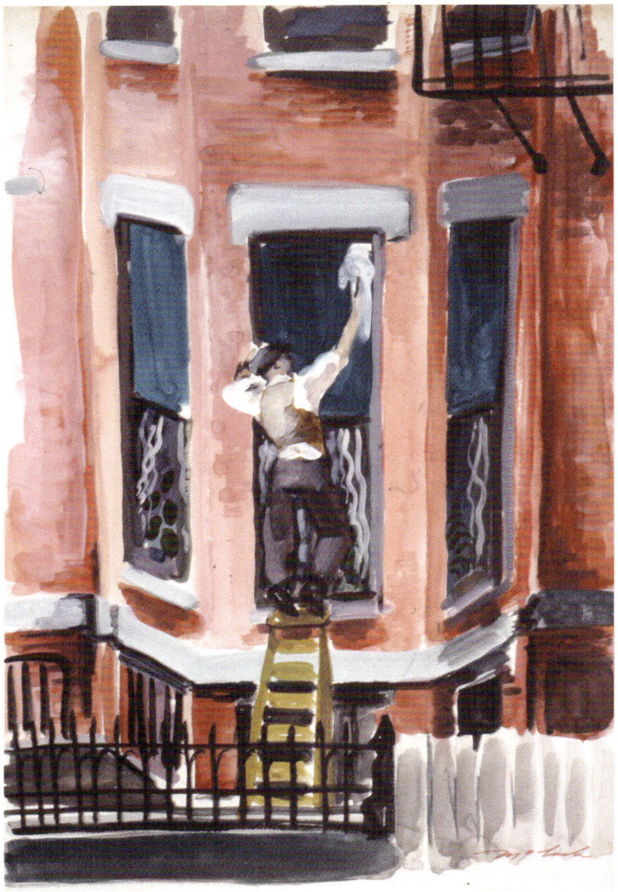

State Street Crossing, 1933
Watercolor on paper, 20 x 14 inches
David John McCosh Memorial Collection

Window Washer, c. 1930
Watercolor on paper, 23 x 14 ½ inches
David John McCosh Memorial Collection

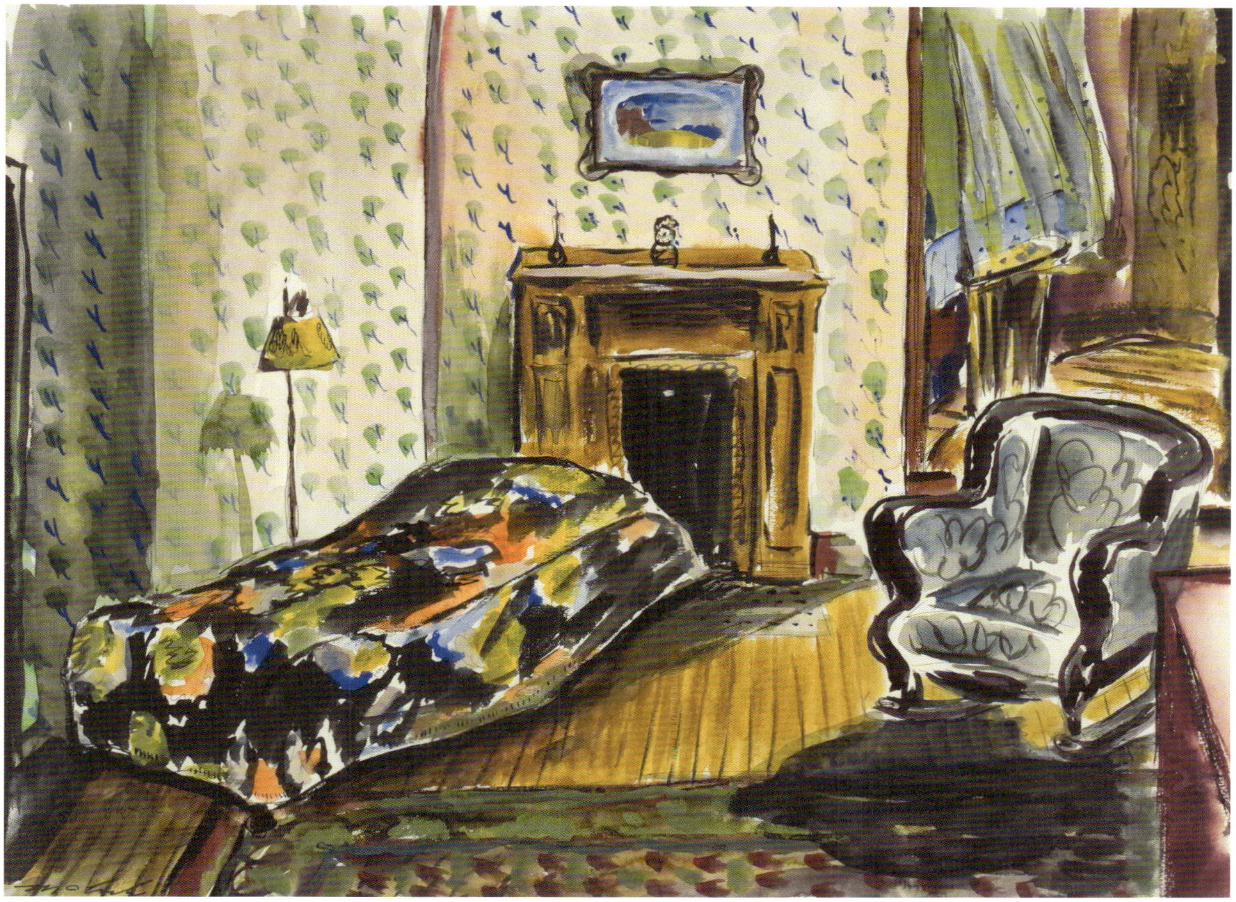

Furnished Room, Chicago, c. 1930
Watercolor on paper, 16 x 21 ¼ inches
David John McCosh Memorial Collection

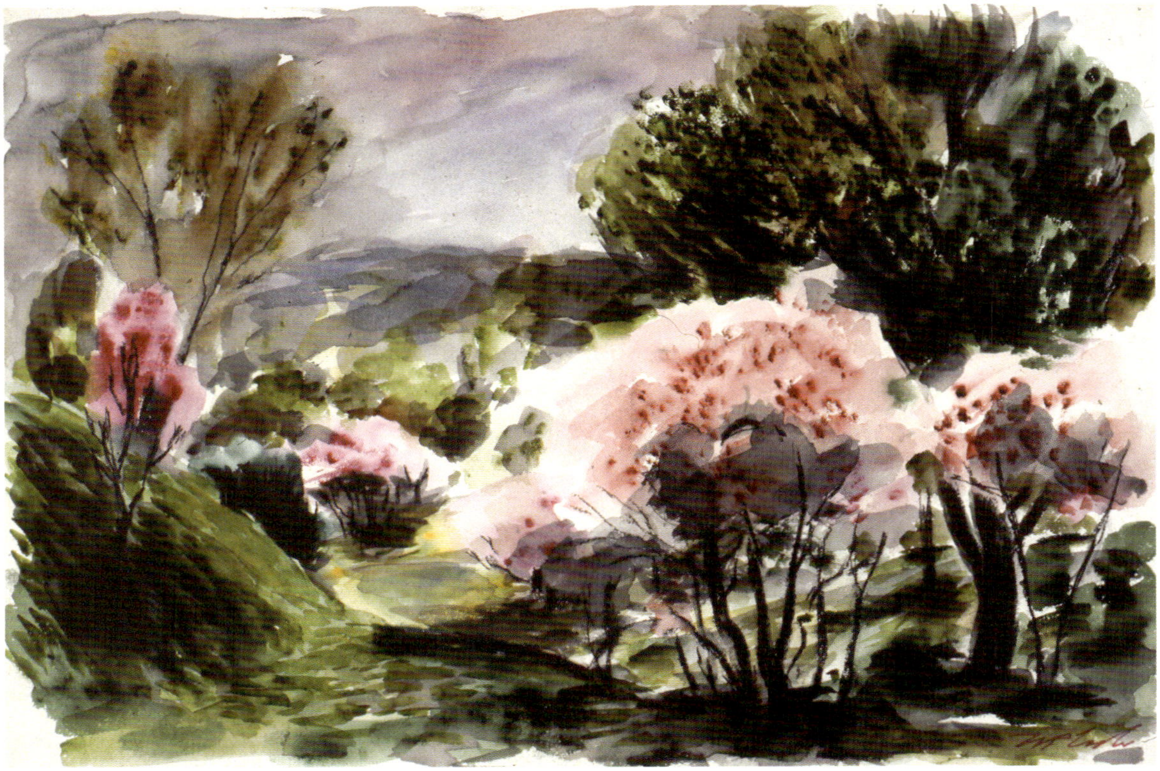

Trees in Bloom, n.d.
Watercolor on paper, 13 7⁄8 x 20 inches
David John McCosh Memorial Collection

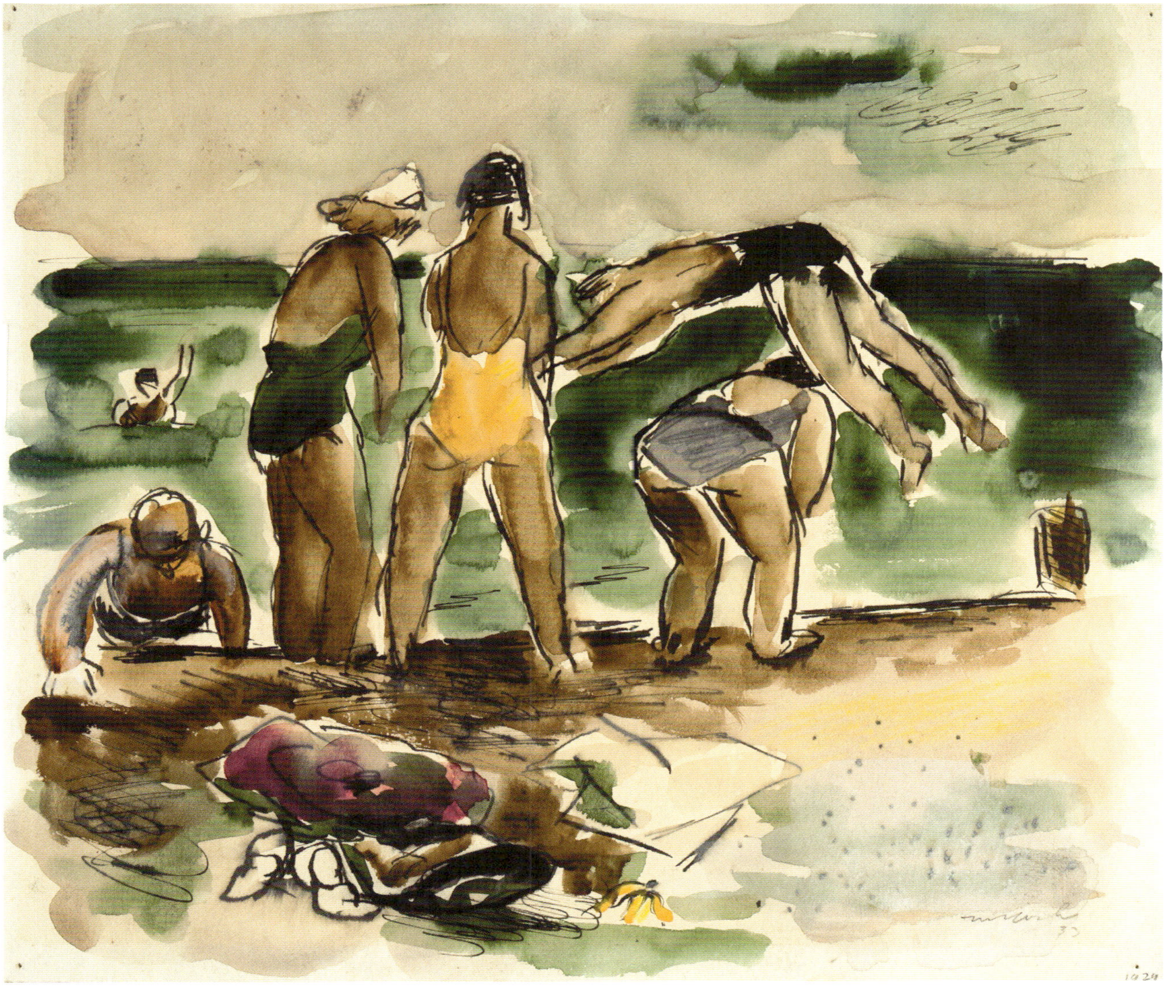

Lakeshore Swimmers in December, 1933
Watercolor and ink on paper, 9 ¾ x 11 ¼ inches
Jordan Schnitzer Museum of Art

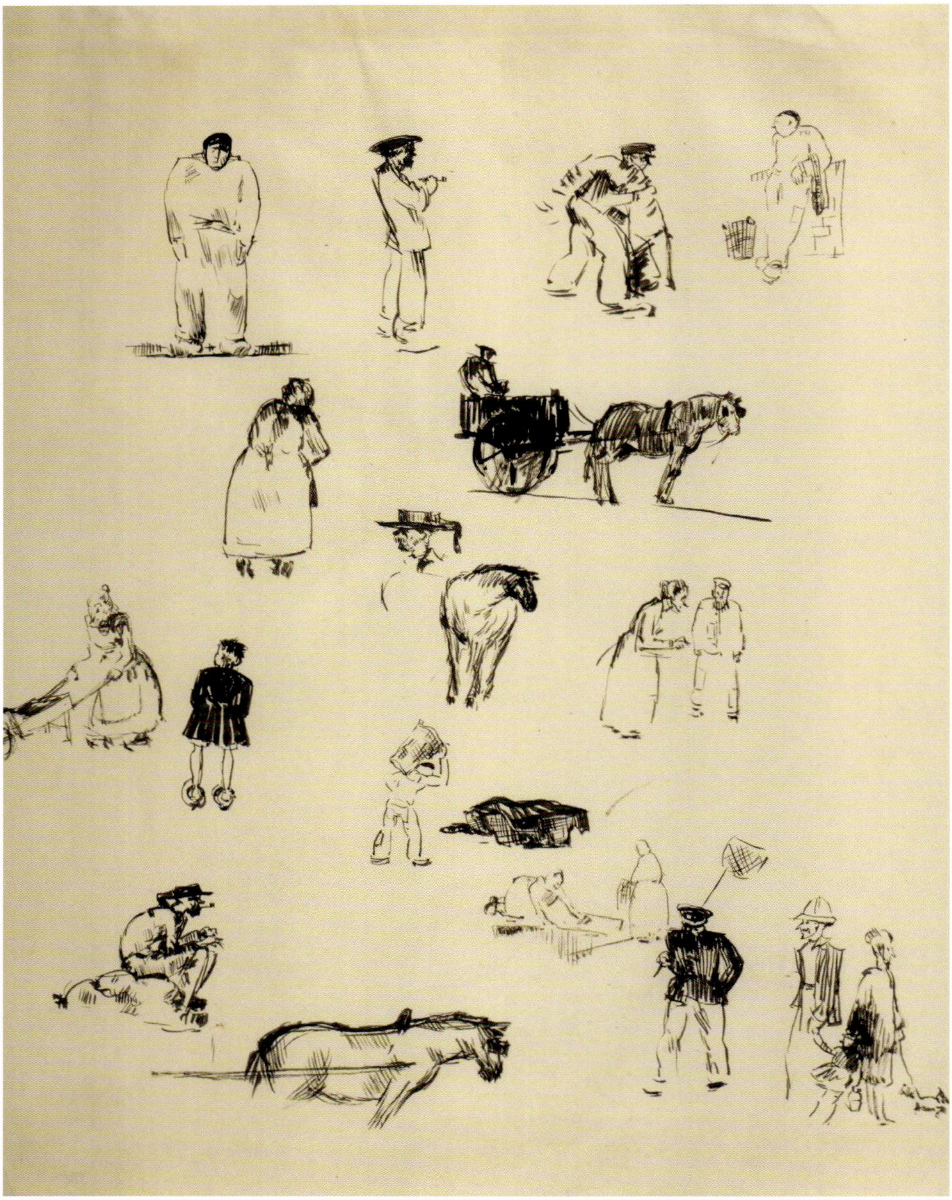

Untitled (Figural Studies, France), 1928
Ink on paper, 10 ½ x 8 ⅛ inches
David John McCosh Memorial Collection

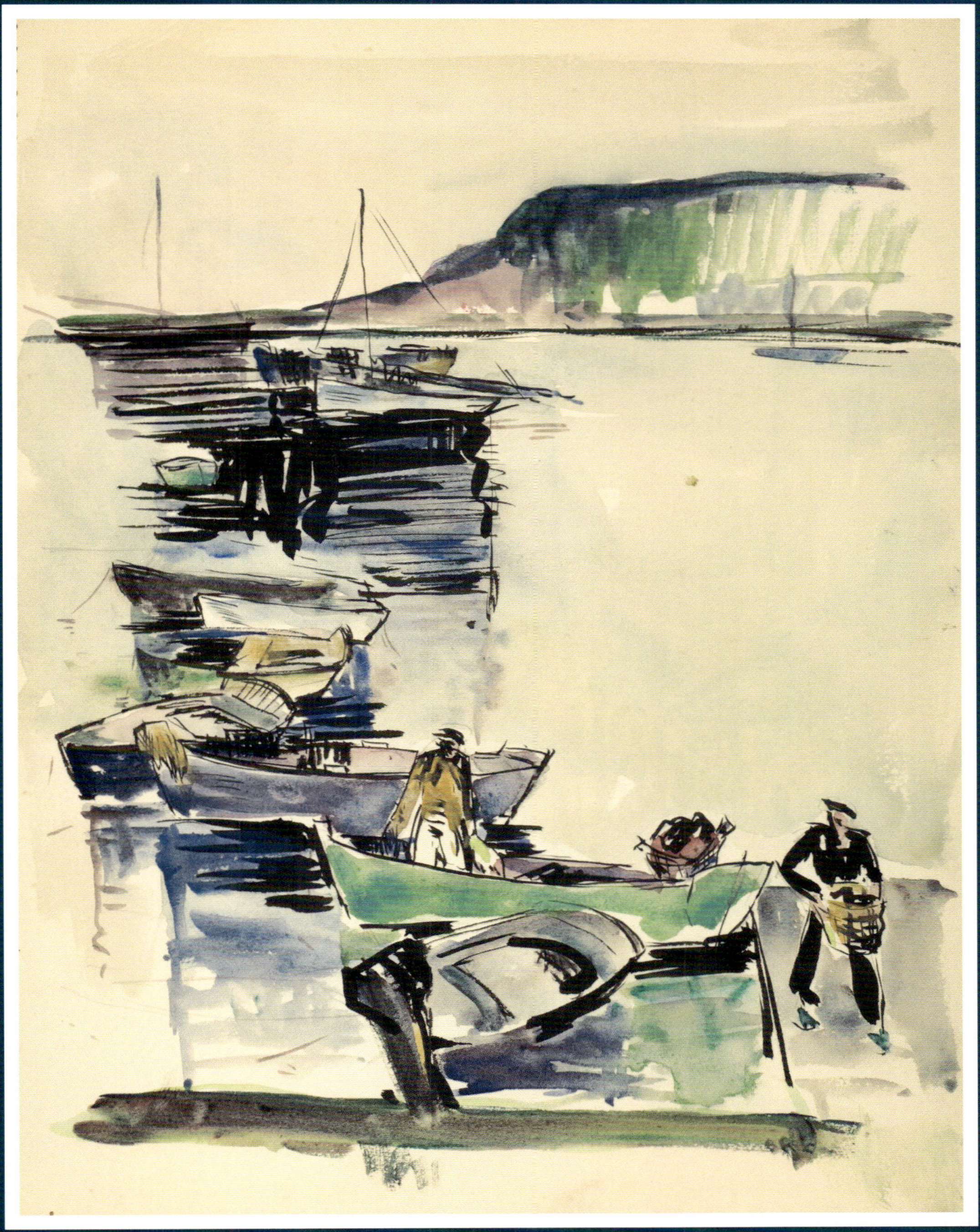

Watercolor Sketch from Roscoff, France, 1928
Sketchbook #3, 10½ x 8 inches
David John McCosh Memorial Archive

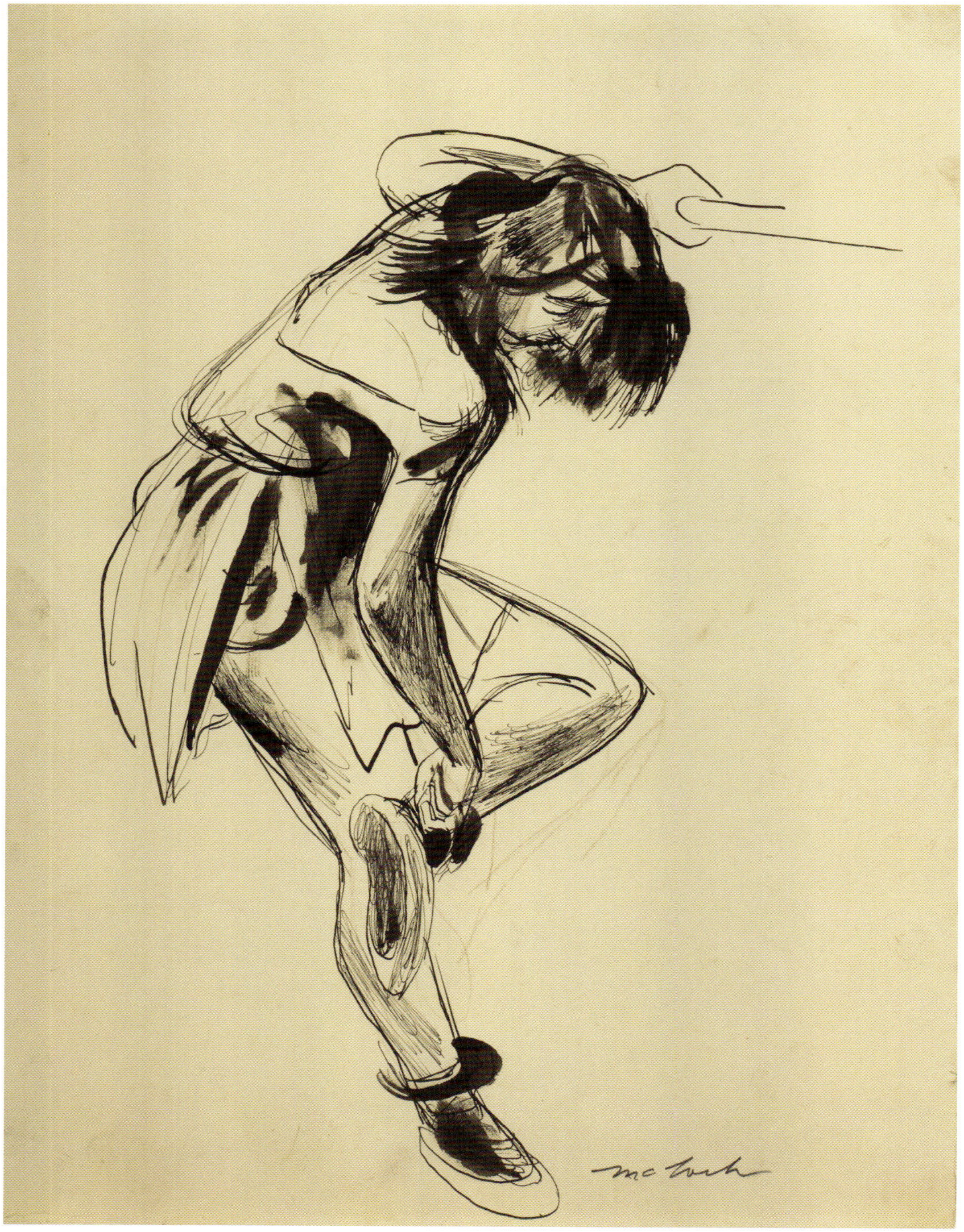

Untitled (Dancer at Barre), n.d.
Ink on paper, 12 ½ x 9 ½ inches
David John McCosh Memorial Collection

THE EARLY DRAWINGS

Craig Cheshire

David McCosh is best known today for his drawings, watercolors, and oil paintings of unexpected aspects of everyday places and things, and for luminous color. In McCosh's early work, we see these same concerns at their earliest stage. He seems to have come to drawing and painting predisposed to look for the particular in his subjects, rejecting any kind of generalization. Light and color also seem to have fascinated him from his student days.

One of his earliest surviving drawings is a female nude figure study (page 44) done when he was a student at the Art Institute of Chicago. Life drawings typically are made with heads that are generic or idealized, unidentifiable as particular people. But in this study, McCosh has drawn an actual person. She is an individual with her own character.

Outside of class, he was constantly alert to what was going on around him, and when something struck him as interesting, funny, or telling, he would make quick drawings in his ever-present sketchbook, sometimes to be worked up later. At first, he favored people as subjects, particularly memorable characters. *The Chambermaid* (page 46) is a poignant study of an overworked African American housekeeper who worked in the rooming house where he was living. Her resigned pose stays in the mind.

Gesture and movement is another way the particular is expressed. McCosh's subjects are always doing something in their own way. *Untitled (Dancer at Barre)* (opposite) is balanced on this point of action, making viewers wonder what she will do next.

He found an equivalent in drawing for his other great preoccupations, color and light. This was tone and descriptive line. In *Woman Sewing* (page 47), rich tone fills the space and expresses a contemplative mood. To suggest light, the artist has to see his subject, even if only a head, as occupying a space that fills the entire paper. *Chapin at Work* (page 46) uses only descriptive line to suggest his friend's concentration and somewhat awkward efforts. The implication of color is always present.

Landscapes, with or without figures, are as different from one another as people and offer immense possibilities for investigating nature's forces, light and color. McCosh eventually drew landscapes as avidly as he did people. *Paris, 1928* (page 48), *Along the Fence* (back cover), and *Tent Show* (page 49) are some of his early landscape attempts. Landscape is a particular challenge in drawing because many things can't be effectively described by putting a line around them. Other linear means must be found—just the kind of challenge that McCosh relished. He referred to this as "descriptive drawing," the drawing equivalent for color.

Drawings like these can be used as a springboard for painting. More often than not, they remain what they are: beautiful drawings, each with its own particular character, different from all others.

Craig Cheshire is a Portland-based painter and emeritus professor at Portland State University, and a member of the McCosh Advisory Committee. He studied under David McCosh at the University of Oregon (BA, 1958; MFA in painting, 1961) and enjoyed a close friendship with his mentor.

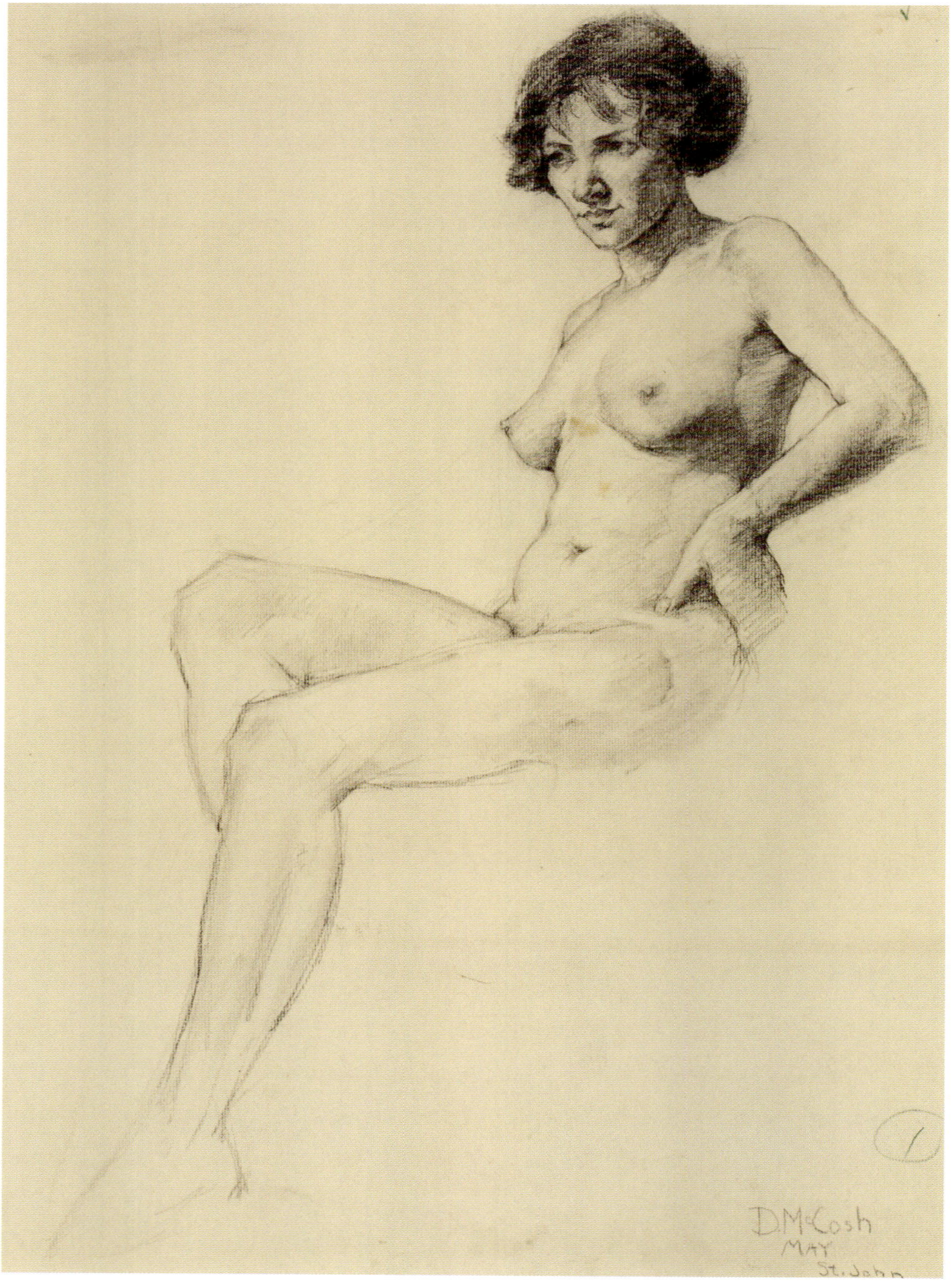

Untitled (Female Model Study from AIC), c. 1925
Pencil on paper, 25 x 19 inches
David John McCosh Memorial Collection

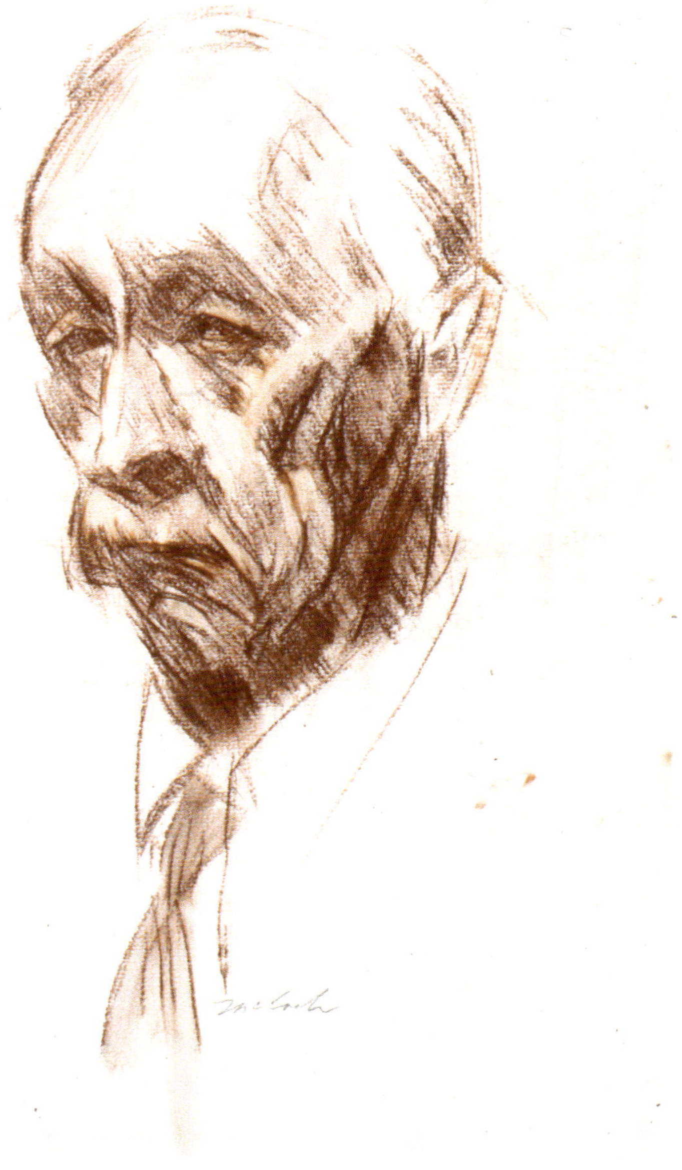

Mr. B. (Portrait of Model at AIC), c. 1930
Conte crayon on paper, 24 x 19 inches
David John McCosh Memorial Collection

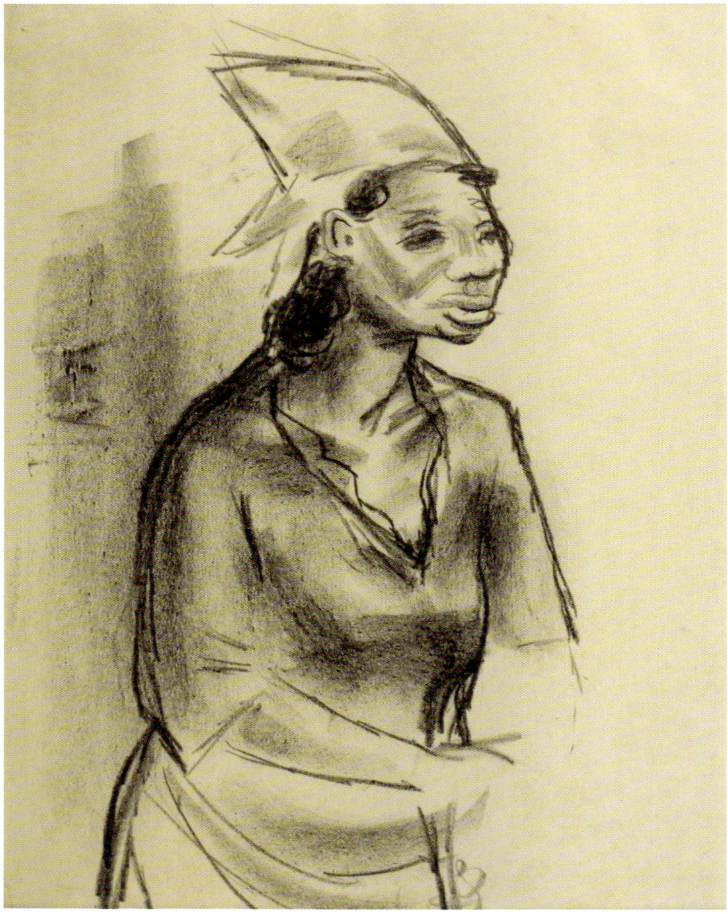

The Chambermaid, 1933
Charcoal and conte crayon on paper, 11 x 8⅜ inches
David John McCosh Memorial Collection

Chapin at Work, c. 1930
Ink on paper,
11 13⁄16 x 17 13⁄16 inches
David John McCosh Memorial Collection

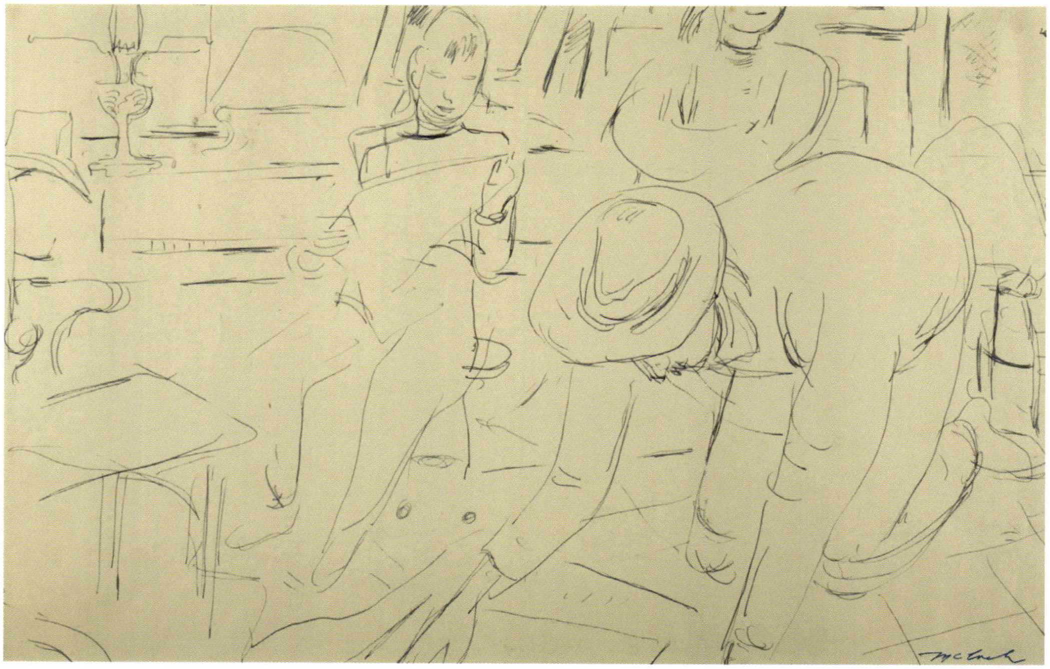

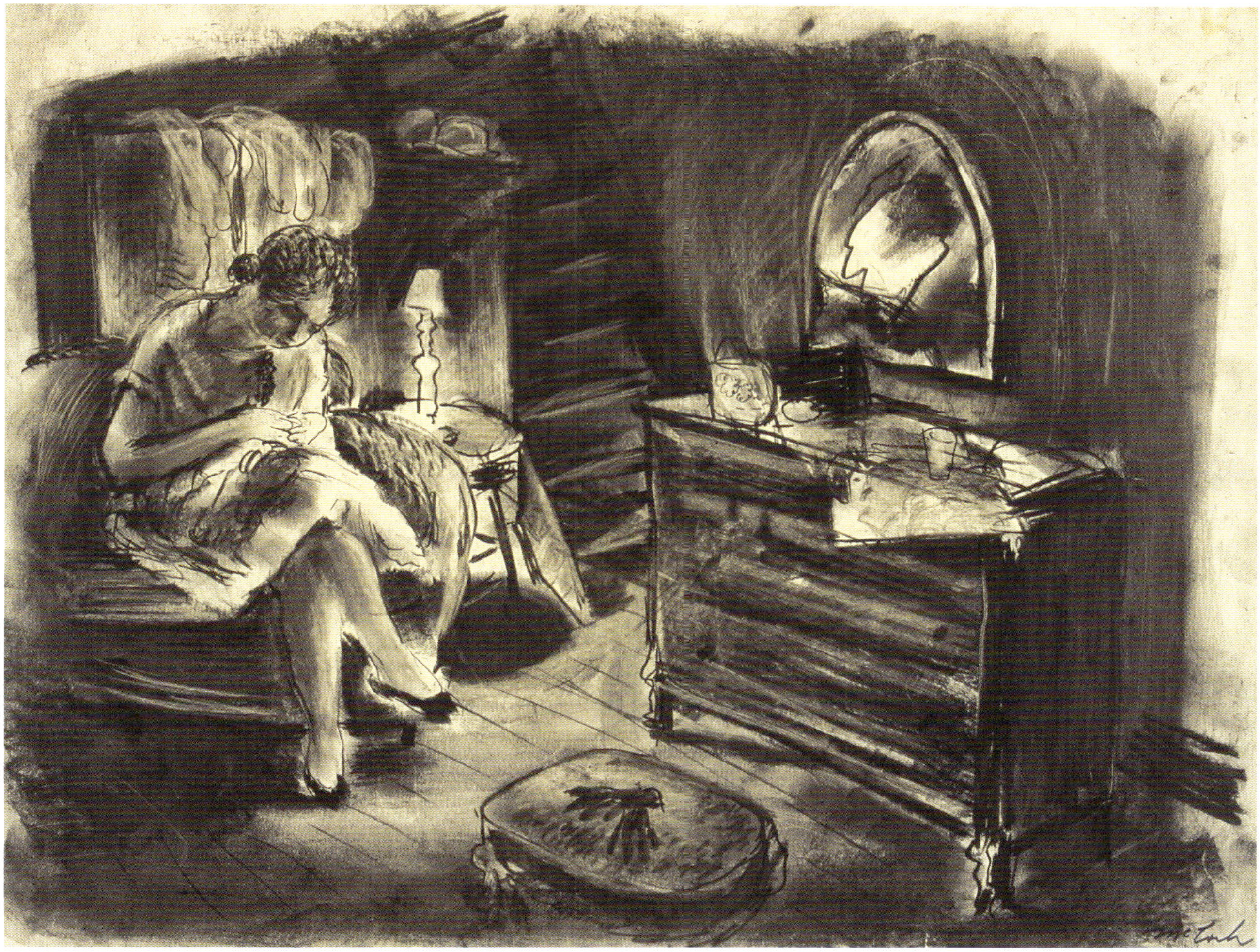

Woman Sewing, c. 1930
Charcoal and ink on paper, 11 x 14 inches
Jordan Schnitzer Museum of Art

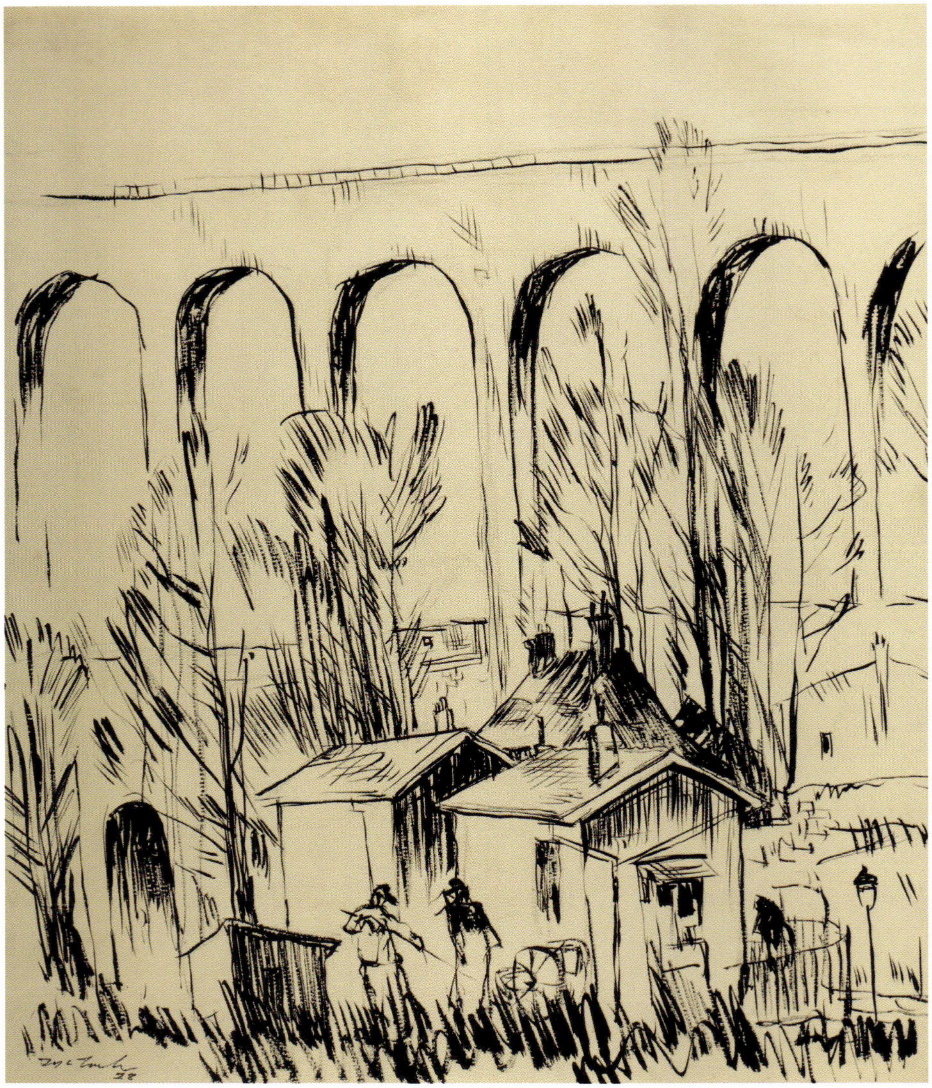

Paris, 1928, 1928
Graphite and ink on paper, 20 1⁄16 x 16 15⁄16 inches
David John McCosh Memorial Collection

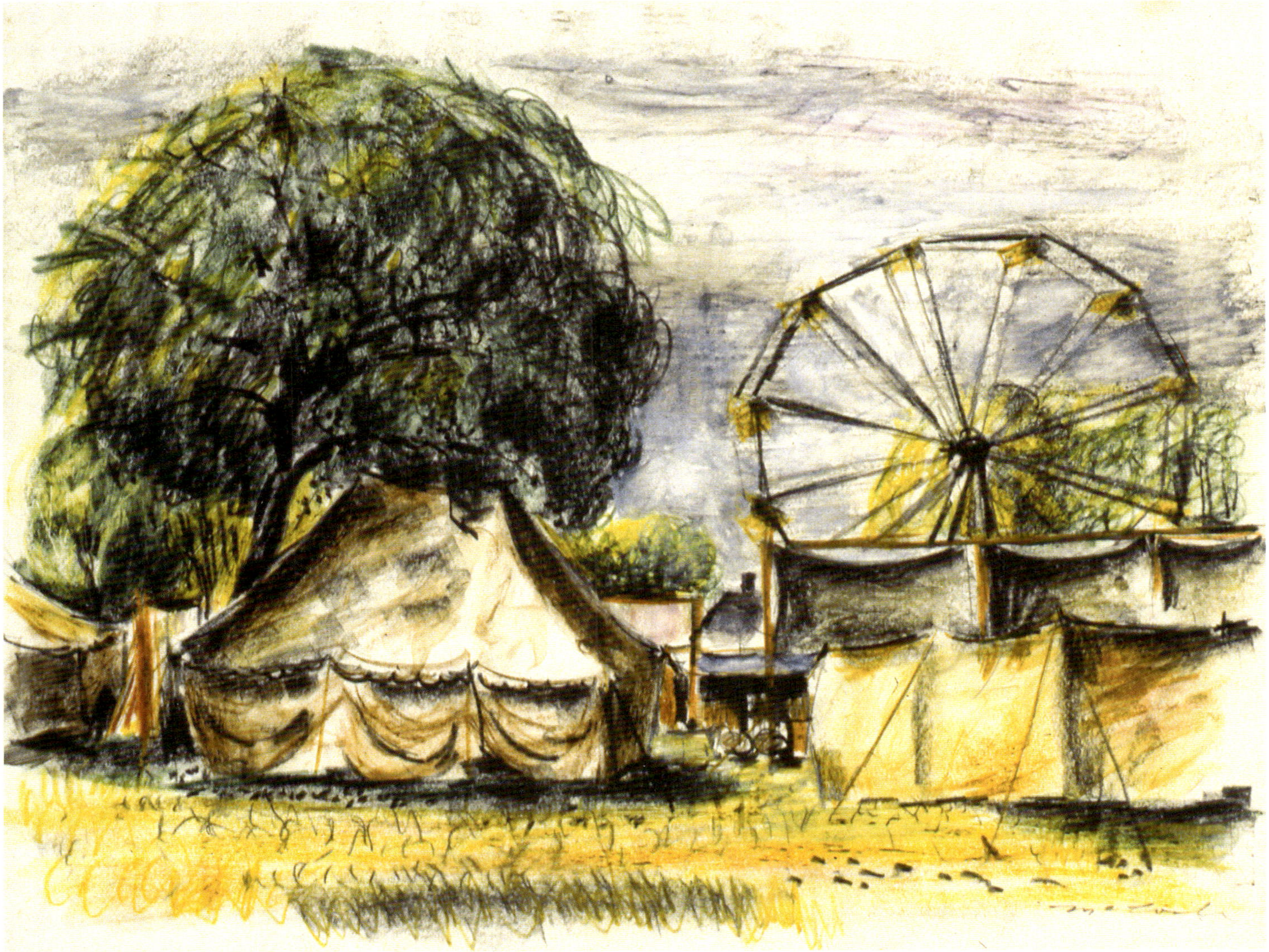

Tent Show, c. 1930
Colored pencil on paper, 10 ¾ x 13 ¾ inches
David John McCosh Memorial Collection

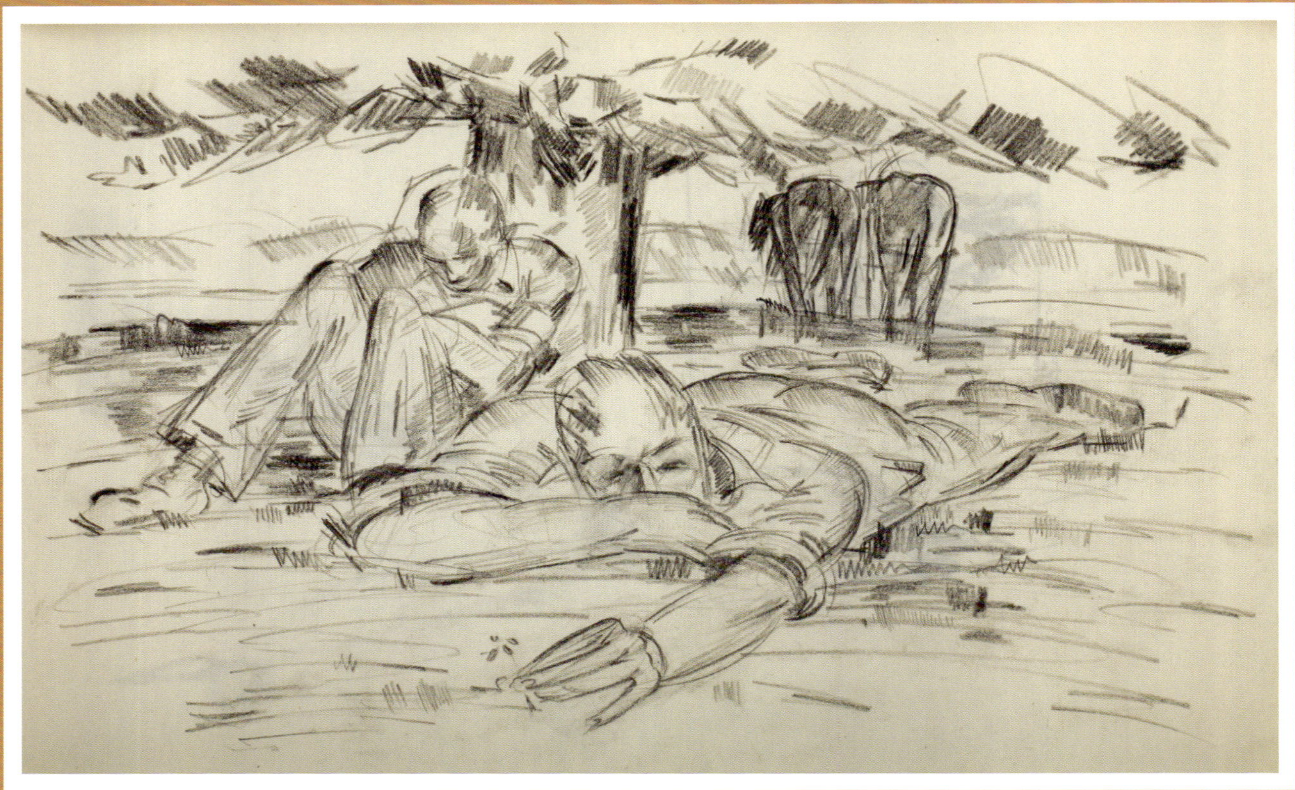

Graphite sketch for Siesta, 1930
Sketchbook #6, 10 ¾ x 14 ½ inches
David John McCosh Memorial Archive

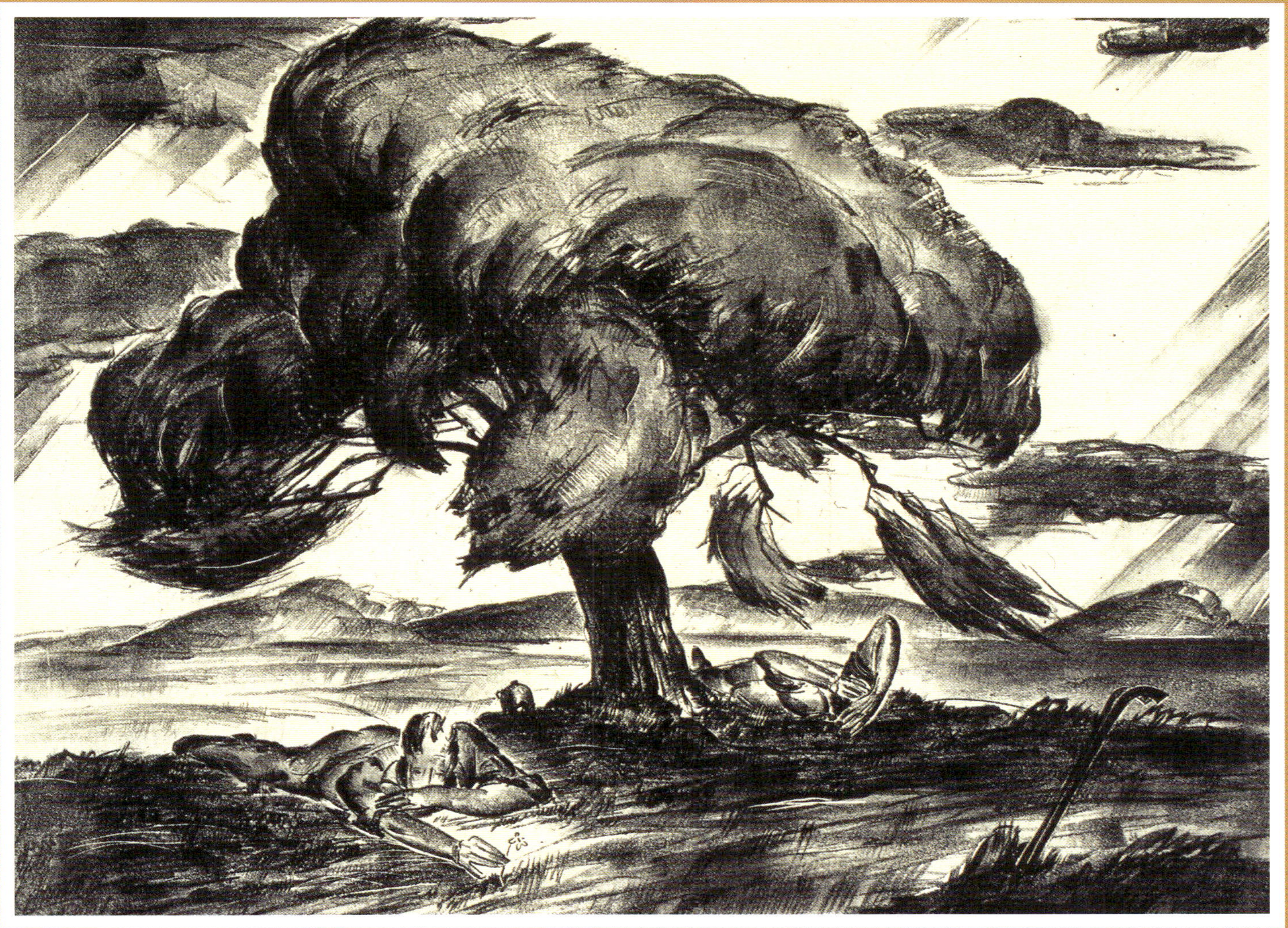

Siesta, 1930
Lithograph, 10 x 13 ¼ inches
Jordan Schnitzer Museum of Art

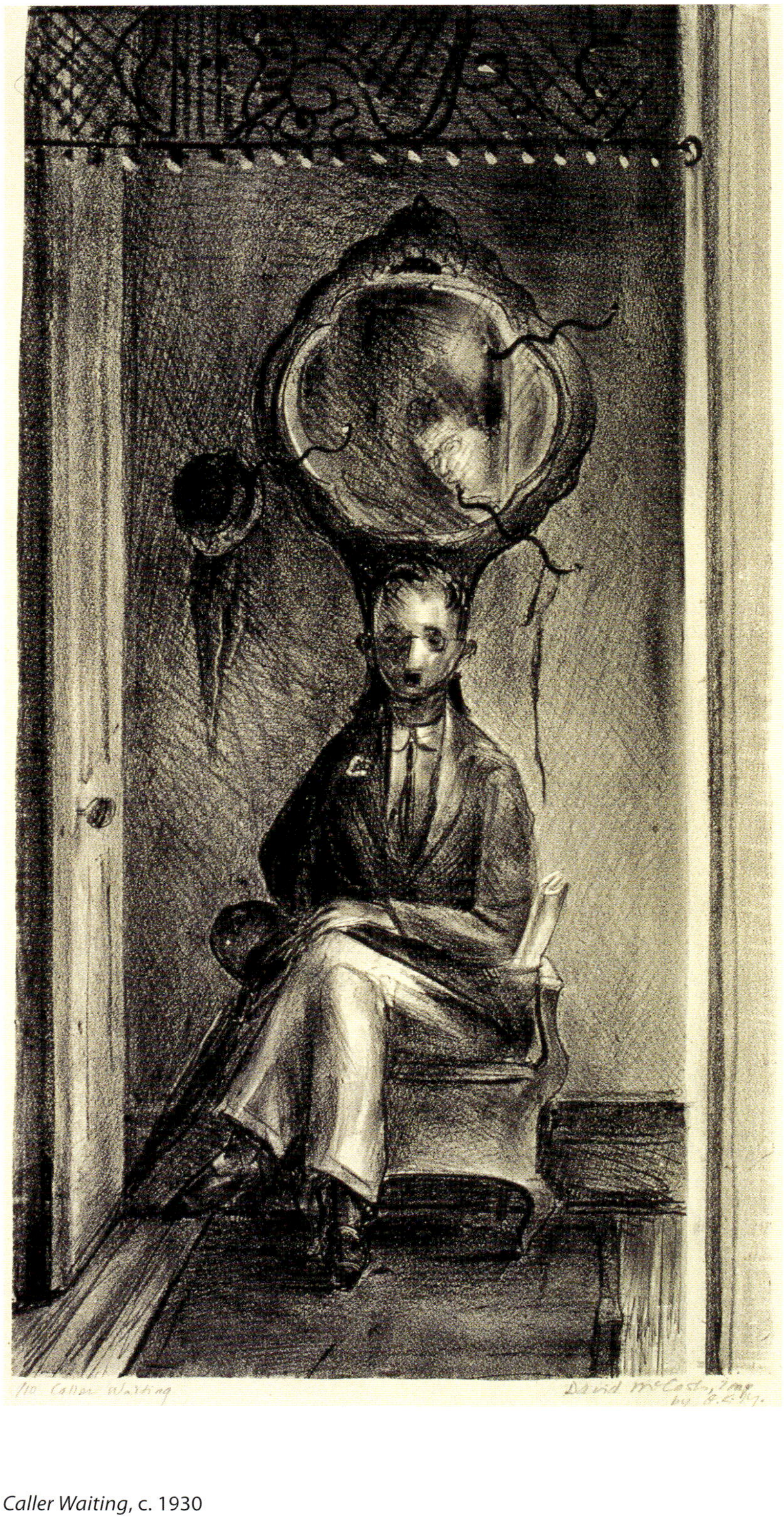

Caller Waiting, c. 1930
Lithograph, 13 x 7 inches
Jordan Schnitzer Museum of Art

THE EARLY LITHOGRAPHS

Aleksandra Globig and June Irene Koehler

The lithographic process was invented by the Bavarian actor and playwright Alois Senefelder in 1798. Though the technique originally flourished as a means to commercially reproduce images for illustrations, by the mid-nineteenth century (later dubbed the "Golden Age of Lithography") it began to be used in more inventive ways by such renowned artists as Daumier and Géricault. By the 1940s, American artist Grant Arnold, who wrote the book *Creative Lithography and How to Do It* (1941), claimed another "Golden Age of Lithography" had emerged thanks to the efforts of artists in the United States, among them the young David McCosh.

Composed in much the same manner as his early drawings and paintings, McCosh's lithographs often feature anonymous figures. In *The El and Babe Ruth* (page 54), the artist has created a simple yet expansive urban scene. Though the industrial buildings and the elevated train loom large, two figures going about their work make the space more accessible.

Other innovative depictions of space in McCosh's early lithographs are of note. Not confined by one particular mode of depiction, he experimented with urban and rural space, indoor and outdoor space. In *Movie Palace* (page 58), figures are shown in motion and at work in their urban environment, illuminated by artificial light. Architectural details on the movie palace and surrounding buildings are meticulously rendered. Conversely, in *Siesta* (page 51), figures are shown lying in repose, one reaching for a daisy, the other contemplating the sky. Lying under a billowing tree, they are bathed in natural sunlight.

In *Storefront in Evening* (page 55), McCosh utilizes the striking contrast of light and dark that the lithographic process affords. While McCosh's placement of the figures allows for the viewer to orient him or herself within this darkened interior, what is contained within the shop windows is not as easily discernible. Hats, scarves and various women's accessories are rendered through subtle silhouettes and shadows, illuminated by harsh artificial light. While *Storefront in Evening* plays with the blurring of the outdoor and indoor, *Caller Waiting* (page 52) presents a solitary figure confined within a cramped interior. The figure waits for his companion beneath an imposing mirror, whose branch-like protrusions mimic the organic lines that make up the metal attachment above it. The reflection of a woman peering around a corner can be seen, giving the shallow composition a sense of greater depth.

As exemplified in these five lithographs and others in his oeuvre, McCosh explored a broad range of subject matter. From urban nightscapes to late afternoon naps in the country, the artist's skill at unifing both figural styles and environmental settings is apparent. These works are striking examples of McCosh's ability to first perceive and then capture the minutest details in the world around him. Rather than limiting his use of lithography to preparatory sketches for oil paintings, McCosh took advantage of the unique expressive and textural possibilities of the medium. Just as the works of the first masters of lithography had achieved the status of autonomous works of art, McCosh's lithographs can be appreciated as finished works in their own right.

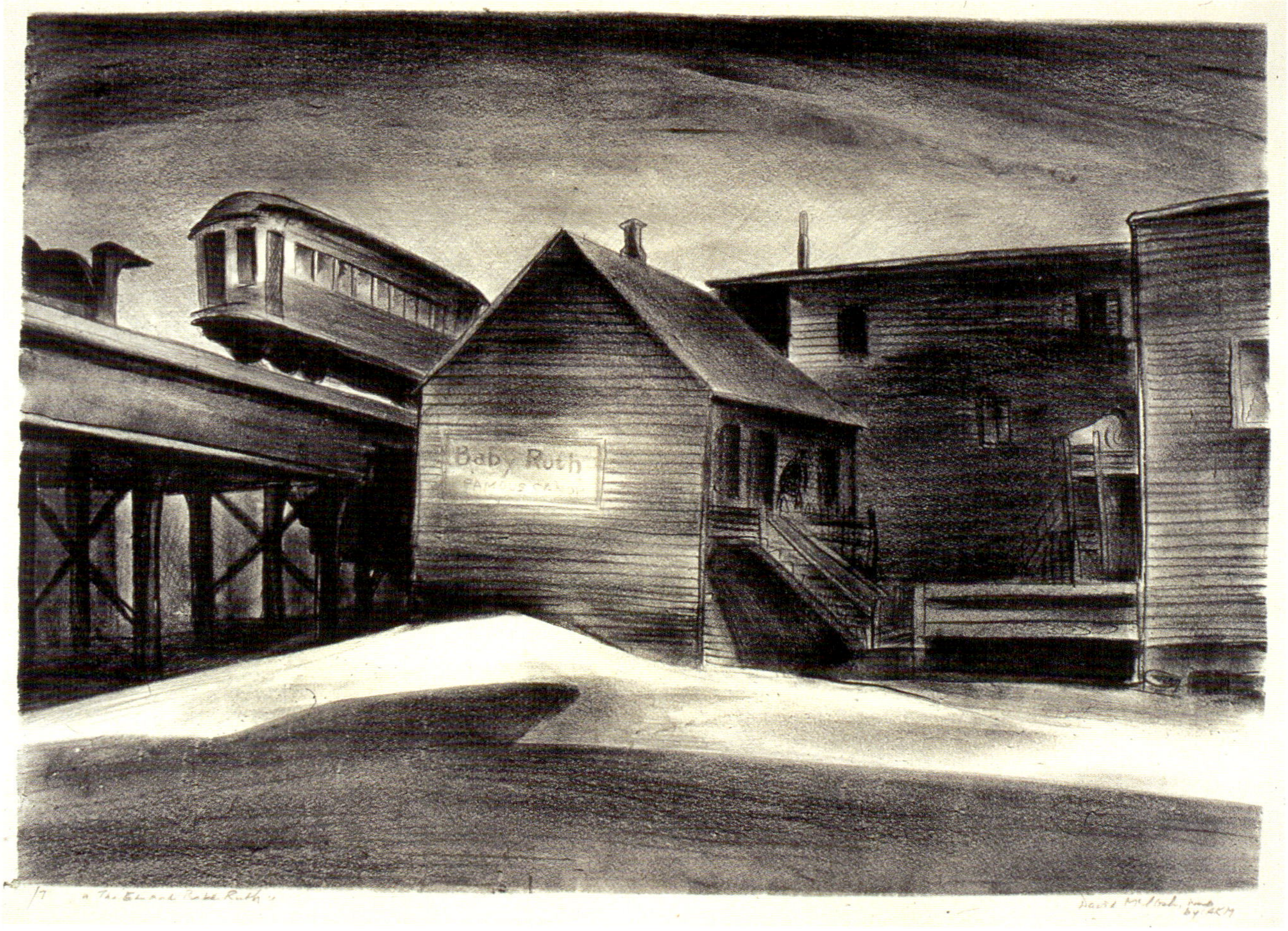

The El and Babe Ruth, c. 1930
Lithograph, 11 x 15 inches
Jordan Schnitzer Museum of Art

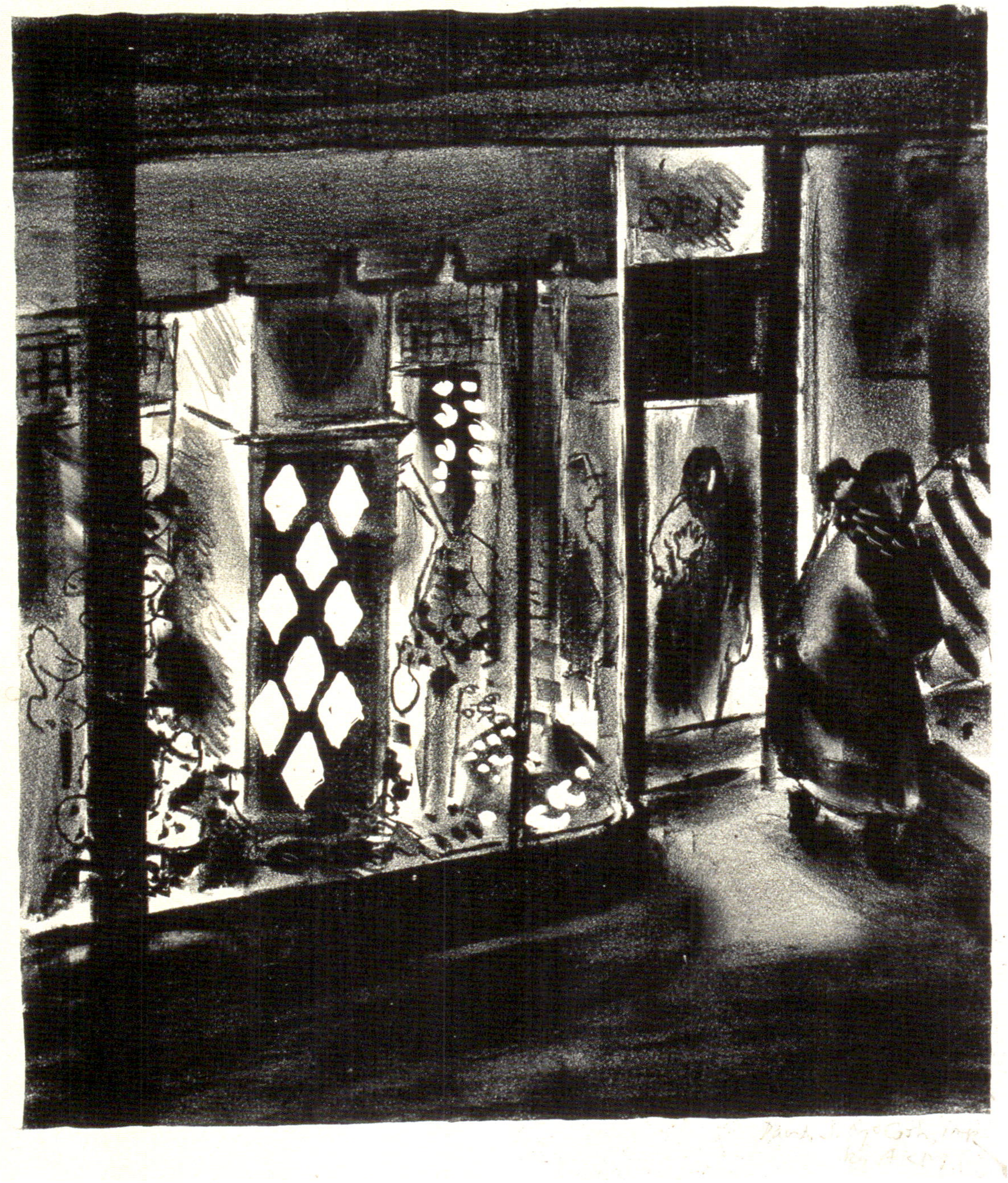

Storefront in Evening, c. 1930
Lithograph, 10 x 8 ½ inches
Jordan Schnitzer Museum of Art

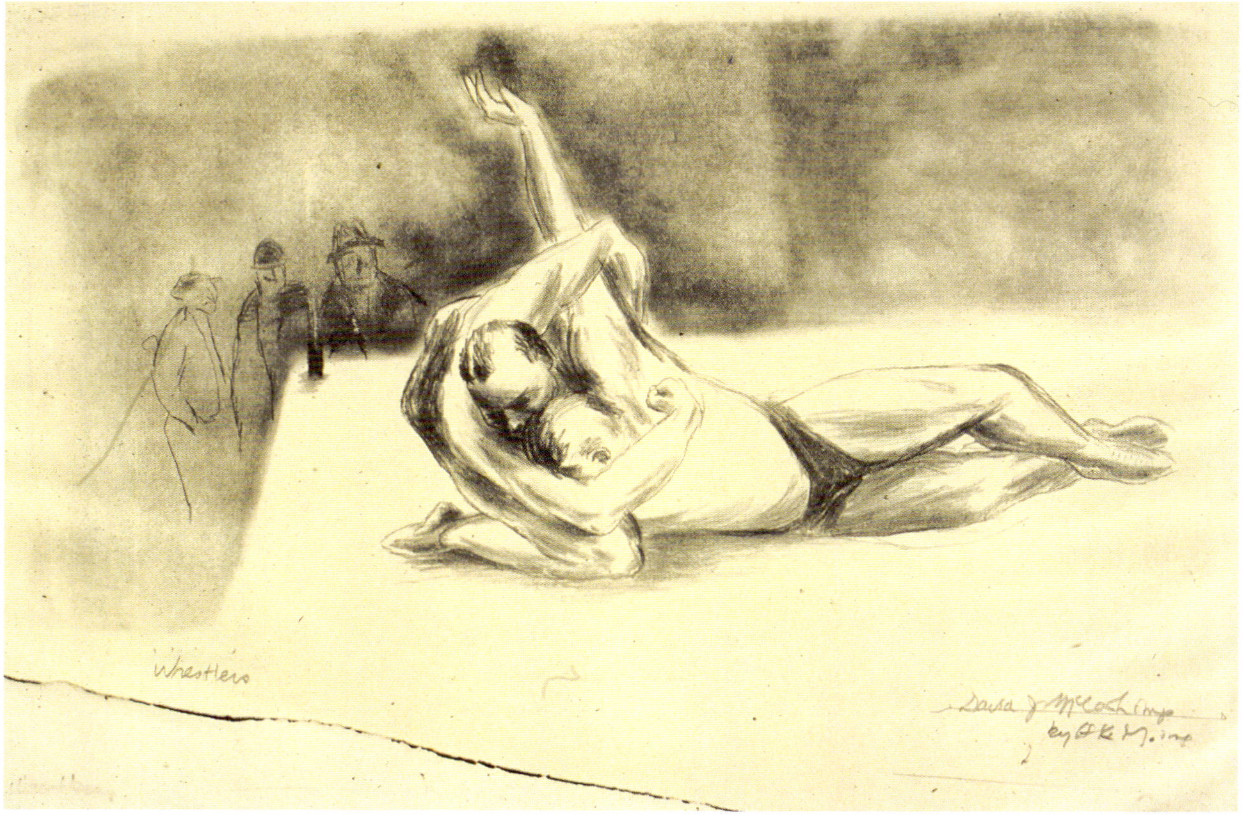

Wrestlers, c. 1930
Lithograph, 5 ½ x 12 inches
Jordan Schnitzer Museum of Art

Next page

Gangster's Funeral I, c. 1930
Lithograph, 10 13⁄16 x 15 inches
Jordan Schnitzer Museum of Art

Gangster's Funeral II, c. 1930
Lithograph, 10 15⁄16 x 15 inches
Jordan Schnitzer Museum of Art

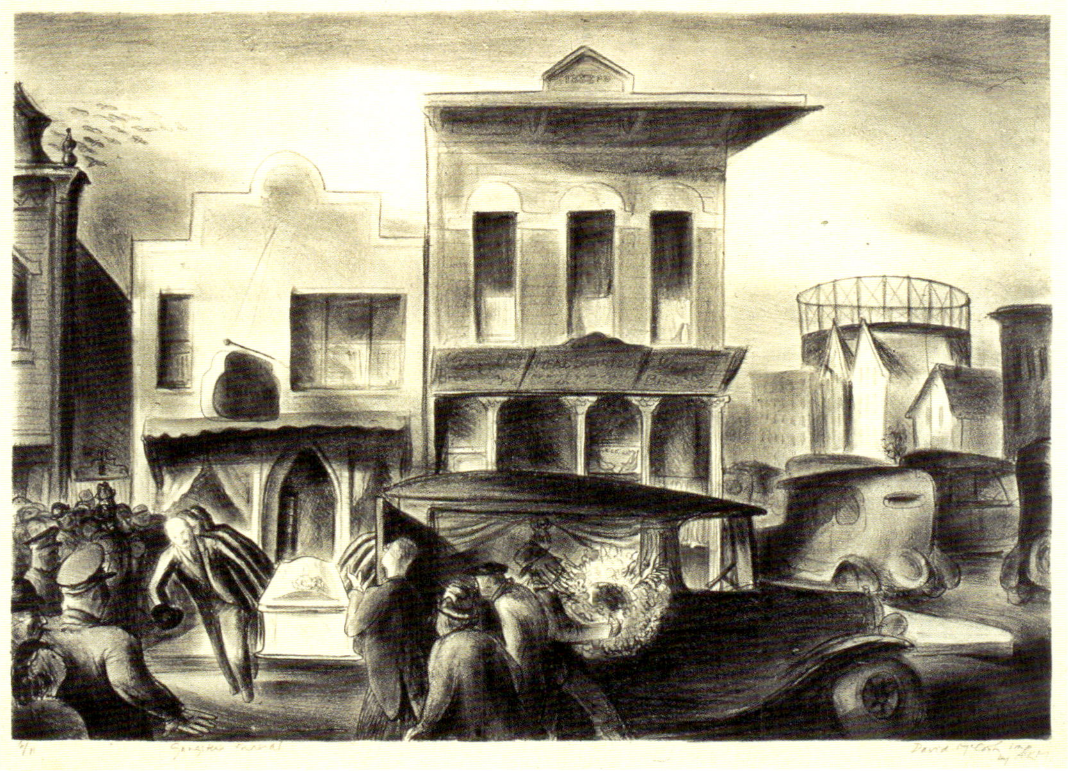

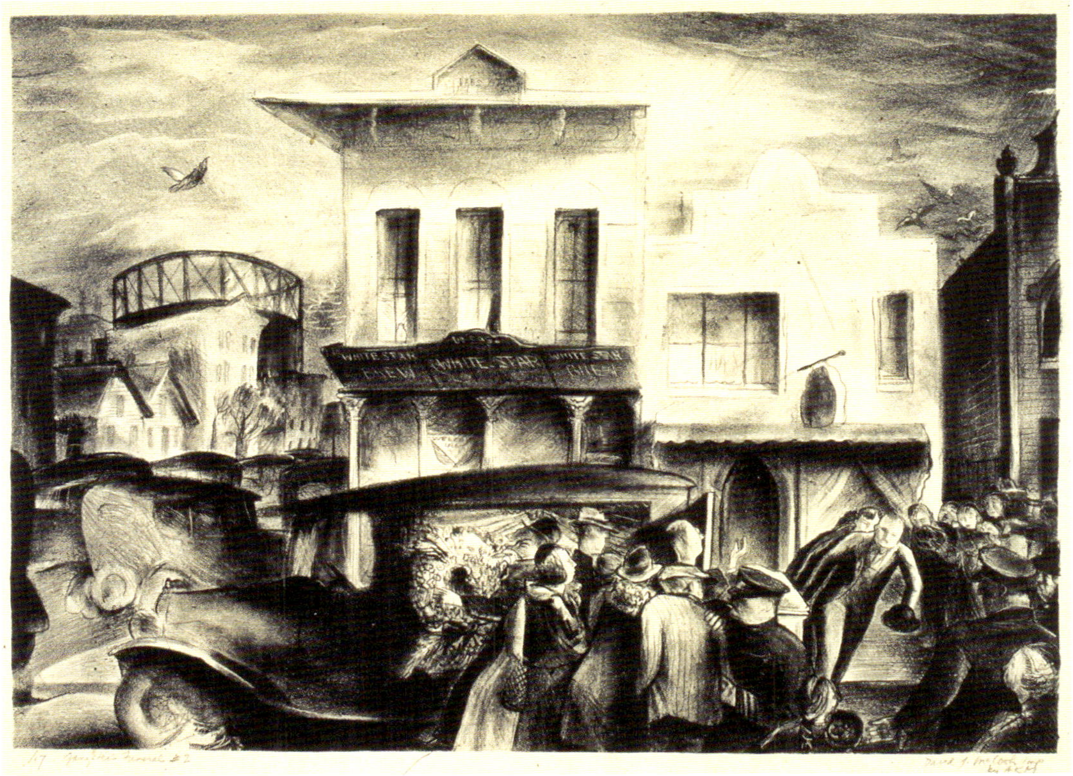
WHITE STAR

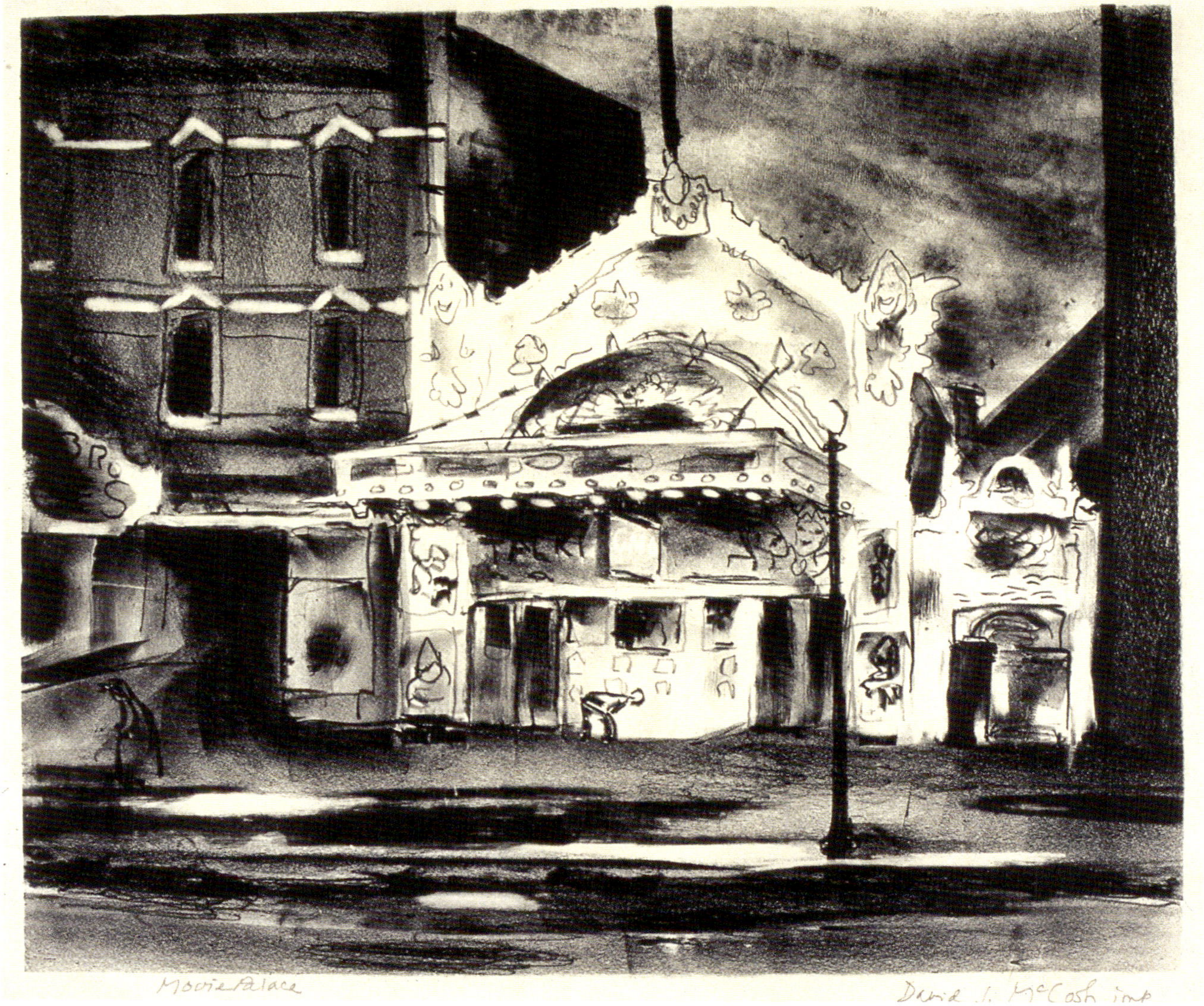

Movie Palace, c. 1930
Lithograph, 9 x 10 ½ inches
Jordan Schnitzer Museum of Art

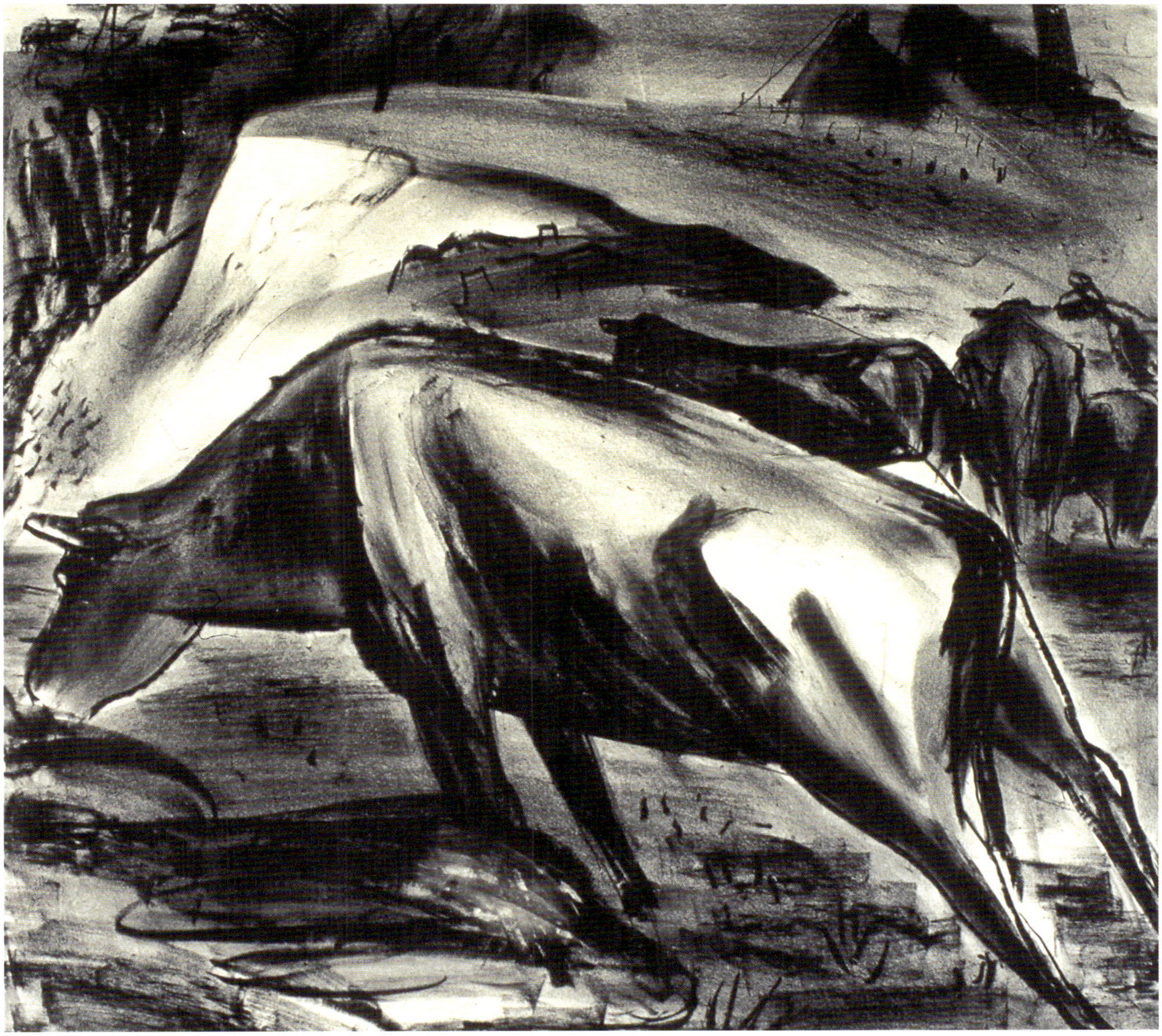

Farm Animals, c. 1930
Lithograph, 11 ¾ x 12 ¾ inches
Jordan Schnitzer Museum of Art

THE MAKING OF DAVID McCOSH: EARLY PAINTINGS, DRAWINGS, AND PRINTS

Exhibition Checklist

Works are listed by lending institution and then by medium and date.
All dimensions are in inches, height x width.

Cedar Rapids Museum of Art
Cedar Rapids, Iowa

The Prodigal Son, 1927
Oil on canvas, 36 ½ x 40 ¾
Museum Purchase
28.1

Pont Marie — Paris, c. 1930
Oil on canvas, 19 ⅛ x 24
On loan from Cedar Rapids Chamber of Commerce
L1983.15.6

Private Collection

The Bachelor, 1932
Oil on canvas, 25 x 30
L2011:15.1

Smithsonian American Art Museum
Washington, D.C.

Woman Ironing, 1931
Oil on canvas, 25 x 30
Gift of Anne Kutka McCosh
1986.89

Wayne State University Art Collection
Detroit, Michigan

Girl Sewing, 1931
Oil on canvas, 30 x 25
Gift of Anne Kutka McCosh
UAC2780

The Foreman, 1932
Oil on canvas, 30 ¼ x 20
Gift of Anne Kutka McCosh
UAC2779

Jordan Schnitzer Museum of Art

OIL PAINTINGS

L'Aquarelliste (Painting of Francis Chapin), c. 1927
Oil on canvas, 23 ¼ x 19 ¼
Gift of Anne Kutka McCosh
1985:14.2

The White Mill, c. 1929
Oil on canvas, 30 x 40
Gift of Anne Kutka McCosh
1990:2.2

Gangster's Funeral, c. 1930
Oil on canvas, 25 x 30
Gift of Anne Kutka McCosh
1985:14.3

Late Afternoon, Early Fall, 1933
Oil on masonite, 26 ½ x 30 ½
Gift of UO Foundation
1990:2.3

WATERCOLORS

Reflections, France, c. 1930
Watercolor on paper, 14 ¾ x 11
Gift of Anne Kutka McCosh
1990:2.11

Deeploma O'Litho, 1932
Watercolor and pencil on paper, 18 ½ x 12
Gift of Matthew C. Collins in memory of Persis Weaver Robertson
2011:7.1

Lakeshore Swimmers in December, 1933
Watercolor and ink on paper, 9 ¾ x 11 ¼
Gift of Anne Kutka McCosh
1990:2.16

The Reservoir, 1934
Watercolor, ink, and charcoal on paper, 14 ½ x 23
Gift of Anne Kutka McCosh
1990:2.18

Woman Sewing, c. 1930
Charcoal and ink on paper, 11 x 14
Gift of Anne Kutka McCosh
1990:2.31

LITHOGRAPHS

Beach Games, c. 1930
Lithograph, 10 x 12 ½
Gift of Anne Kutka McCosh
1990:2.73

Bicyclers, c. 1930
Lithograph, 9 x 9 ½
Gift of Anne Kutka McCosh
1990:2.122

Caller Waiting, c. 1930
Lithograph, 13 x 7
Gift of Anne Kutka McCosh
1990:2.67

The El and Babe Ruth, c. 1930
Lithograph, 11 x 15
Gift of Anne Kutka McCosh
1990:2.91

Farm Animals, c. 1930
Lithograph, 11 ¾ x 12 ¾
Gift of Anne Kutka McCosh
1990:2.116

Farm Home and Bridge, c. 1930
Lithograph, 8 x 12 ¼
Gift of Anne Kutka McCosh
1990:2.106

Flood, c. 1930
Lithograph, 10 x 14
Gift of Anne Kutka McCosh
1990:2.107

Gangster's Funeral I, c. 1930
Lithograph, 10 13/16 x 15
Gift of Anne Kutka McCosh
1990:2.94

Gangster's Funeral II, c. 1930
Lithograph, 10 15/16 x 15
Gift of Anne Kutka McCosh
1990:2.95

Late Night in Chicago, c. 1930
Lithograph, 8 x 11 ½
Gift of Anne Kutka McCosh
1990:2.83

Loggers at Work, c. 1930
Lithograph, 9 ⅜ x 6 ⅞
Gift of Anne Kutka McCosh
1990:2.101

Movie Palace, c. 1930
Lithograph, 9 x 10 ½
Gift of Anne Kutka McCosh
1990:2.81

Old House, Bertram, Iowa, c. 1930
Lithograph, 11 x 14
Gift of Anne Kutka McCosh
1990:2.108

Performers, c. 1930
Lithograph, 8 ½ x 7
Gift of Anne Kutka McCosh
1990:2.62

Return Trip, c. 1930
Lithograph, 9 x 12
Gift of Anne Kutka McCosh
1990:2.92

Sleeping Man, c. 1930
Lithograph, 5 x 8
Gift of Anne Kutka McCosh
1990:2.63

Store Front in Evening, c. 1930
Lithograph, 10 x 8 ½
Gift of Anne Kutka McCosh
1990:2.84

Street Scene, c. 1930
Lithograph, 5 3⁄16 x 11 11⁄16
Gift of Anne Kutka McCosh
1990:2.98

Summer Art Colony, c. 1930
Lithograph, 11 ½ x 16
Gift of Anne Kutka McCosh
1990:2.117

Sun Bath, c. 1930
Lithograph, 4 ½ x 6 ½
Gift of Anne Kutka McCosh
1990:2.75

Wrestlers, c. 1930
Lithograph, 5 ½ x 12
Gift of Anne Kutka McCosh
1990: 2.123

Siesta, 1930
Lithograph, 10 x 13 ¼
Gift of Anne Kutka McCosh
1990:2.100

Cedar Valley, 1932
Lithograph, 9 x 13
Gift of Anne Kutka McCosh
1990:2.121

Chape, 1932
Lithograph, 10 ½ x 16
Gift of Anne Kutka McCosh
1990:2.65

Parade, 1933
Lithograph, 12 x 10
Gift of Anne Kutka McCosh
1990:2.93

Lone Rider, n.d.
Lithograph, 10 x 14
Gift of Anne Kutka McCosh
1990:2.120

UO Foundation David John McCosh Memorial Collection

OIL PAINTINGS

Wyoming, 1927
Oil on linen, 20 x 23 ¾
Gift of Anne Kutka McCosh
MMC 186

French Countryside, 1928
Oil on canvas, 20 x 23 ½
Gift of Anne Kutka McCosh
MMC 189

Self-Portrait (Unfinished), 1928
Oil on canvas, 18 x 20
Gift of Anne Kutka McCosh
MMC 202

Mr. B. (Portrait of Model at the Art Institute), 1930
Oil on linen, 20 x 17 ¾
Gift of Anne Kutka McCosh
MMC 180

The Flagman, c.1931-32
Oil on linen, 24 x 20
Gift of Anne Kutka McCosh
MMC 3

The Trombone Player, c. 1932
Oil on linen, 30 x 24 ½
Gift of Anne Kutka McCosh
MMC 170

Concentration (Portrait of Anne McCosh), August 1934
Oil on canvas, 18 x 20
Gift of Anne Kutka McCosh
MMC 1

WATERCOLORS

Lake Lucerne, Switzerland, 1928
Watercolor on paper, 20 x 17
Gift of Anne Kutka McCosh
MMC 425

Europe, 1929
Watercolor on paper, 16 ¾ x 20
Gift of Anne Kutka McCosh
MMC 426

Furnished Room, Chicago, c. 1930
Watercolor on paper, 16 x 21 ¼
Gift of Anne Kutka McCosh
MMC 554

Oyster Bay, 1930
Watercolor on paper, 15 ½ x 22 ⅜
Gift of Anne Kutka McCosh
MMC 700

Potted Plant, 1930
Watercolor and graphite on paper, 14 ⅜ x 10 ¼
Gift of Anne Kutka McCosh
MMC 694

Shoppers Resting, 1930
Watercolor on paper, 14 x 22
Gift of Anne Kutka McCosh
MMC 515

Still-Life at Tiffany Foundation, 1930
Watercolor on paper, 15 ⅜ x 22 ⅜
Gift of Anne Kutka McCosh
MMC 702

Window Washer, c. 1930
Watercolor and gouache on paper, 23 x 14 ½
Gift of Anne Kutka McCosh
MMC 1307

Tombstones, Oak Hill Cemetery — Cedar Rapids, 1932
Watercolor on paper, 15 x 22
Gift of Anne Kutka McCosh
MMC 543

State Street Crossing, 1933
Watercolor on paper, 20 x 14
Gift of Anne Kutka McCosh
MMC 687

Steeples, 1933
Watercolor on paper, 19 x 14
Gift of Anne Kutka McCosh
MMC 681

Jockeys, 1934
Watercolor on paper, 15 ⅜ x 22 ½
Gift of Anne Kutka McCosh
MMC 516

Willow Springs, CCC Camp, Illinois, 1934
Watercolor on paper, 14 x 19
Gift of Anne Kutka McCosh
MMC 1306

Trees in Bloom, n.d.
Watercolor on paper, 13 ⅞ x 20
Gift of Anne Kutka McCosh
MMC 704

DRAWINGS

Untitled (Male Model Study from AIC), c. 1924
Pencil on paper, 25 x 19
Gift of Anne Kutka McCosh
MMC 8080

Untitled (Female Model Study from AIC), c. 1925
Pencil on paper, 25 x 19
Gift of Anne Kutka McCosh
MMC 8089

Untitled (Skeletal Study from AIC), c. 1925
Pencil on paper, 24 ½ x 18 ⅝
Gift of Anne Kutka McCosh
MMC 8117

Preliminary Sketch for *The Prodigal Son*, 1927
Graphite on paper, 17 ½ x 18 ¾
Gift of Anne Kutka McCosh
MMC 8076

Paris, 1928, 1928
Graphite and ink on paper, 20 1⁄16 x 16 15⁄16
Gift of Anne Kutka McCosh
MMC 384

Untitled (Figural Studies, France), 1928
Ink on paper, 10 ½ x 8 ⅛
Gift of Anne Kutka McCosh
MMC 1284

Untitled (Figural Studies, France), 1928
Ink on paper, 10 ½ x 8 ⅛
Gift of Anne Kutka McCosh
MMC 1299

Untitled (Figural Studies, France), 1928
Ink on paper, 10 ½ x 8 ⅛
Gift of Anne Kutka McCosh
MMC 1364

Chapin at Work, c. 1930
Ink on paper, 11 13⁄16 x 17 13⁄16
Gift of Anne Kutka McCosh
MMC 507

Gangster's Funeral, c. 1930
Ink on paper, 14 x 18 ⅞
Gift of Anne Kutka McCosh
MMC 686

Mr. B. (Portrait of Model at the Art Institute), c. 1930
Conte crayon on paper, 24 x 19
Gift of Anne Kutka McCosh
MMC 712

"Peavy'd be a good man if he wasn't so near-sighted." c. 1930
Chalk on paper, 19 x 14
Gift of Anne Kutka McCosh
MMC 531

Tent Show, c.1930
Colored pencil on paper, 10 ¾ x 13 ¾
Gift of Anne Kutka McCosh
MMC 653

Along the Fence, July 4, 1930
Charcoal on paper, 14 ⅜ x 10 ¼
Gift of Anne Kutka McCosh
MMC 693

The Chambermaid, 1933
Charcoal and conte crayon, 11 x 8 ⅜
Gift of Anne Kutka McCosh
MMC 719

Policeman, n.d.
Charcoal and graphite on paper, 11 x 8 ½
Gift of Anne Kutka McCosh
MMC 1359

Untitled (Dancer at Barre), n.d.
Ink on paper, 12 ½ x 9 ½
Gift of Anne Kutka McCosh
MMC 565

Sketchbook #1 (School of the Art Institute of Chicago), 1927
5 x 7 inches
Gift of Anne Kutka McCosh

Sketchbook #3 (Europe), 1928
10 ½ x 8
Gift of Anne Kutka McCosh

Sketchbook #5 (Europe), 1928
9 ¼ x 7 ½
Gift of Anne Kutka McCosh

Sketchbook #6 (New York), 1930 or 1931
14 ½ x 10 ¾
Gift of Anne Kutka McCosh

Sketchbook #7 (Stone City, Iowa), 1932–33
10 x 7 ¾
Gift of Anne Kutka McCosh

Sketchbook #10 (Chicago World's Fair), 1933
10 x 7 ¾
Gift of Anne Kutka McCosh

Sketchbook #11 (Chicago), 1930–33
10 x 7 ¾
Gift of Anne Kutka McCosh

Sketchbook #12 (Chicago and New York), 1933
10 x 17 ¾
Gift of Anne Kutka McCosh

Sketchbook #17 (Willow Springs, Illinois), 1934
10 x 7 ¾
Gift of Anne Kutka McCosh

CHRONOLOGY OF THE ARTIST'S LIFE

David McCosh regularly exhibited his work in one-man shows, group exhibitions, juried competitions, and regional and national invitationals. This abbreviated chronology lists notable teaching appointments, travels, sabbaticals, public murals, and publications. For a complete exhibition history, visit jsma.uoregon.edu or see *David McCosh* (Eugene, Oregon: University of Oregon Museum of Art, University of Oregon, 1985) by Leonard Buell Kimbrell and *The Sketchbooks of David McCosh* (Eugene, Oregon: University of Oregon Museum of Art, 1994) by Craig Cheshire.

July 11, 1903
Born in Cedar Rapids, Iowa

1922–1923
Pursues undergraduate studies at Coe College, Cedar Rapids, Iowa

1923–1926
Pursues undergraduate studies at the School of the Art Institute of Chicago (AIC)

1927
Spends the summer in Wyoming on a painting trip

1927–1929
Pursues graduate studies at the AIC, during which he spends eight months in Europe on a John Quincy Adams Scholarship for Foreign Travel

1930
Receives Tiffany Foundation Fellowship to spend the summer painting at Oyster Bay, Long Island, where he meets Anne Kutka; works with master printmaker Bolton Brown in Chicago

1931
Rooms with Herbert Ferber Silvers in New York City in the winter and spends the summer working in Grant Arnold's lithography studio in Woodstock, New York

1932
Serves as director and instructor at the Davenport Municipal Art Gallery in Davenport, spends the summer teaching at Grant Wood's Stone City Art Colony, and begins teaching lithography at the AIC

1933
Paints mural in the Hall of Social Science for "A Century of Progress" International Exposition in Chicago; resumes teaching position at Stone City Art Colony in the summer

1934
Spends March and April at Camp Chicago Lemont in Willow Springs, Illinois, documenting the Civilian Conservation Corps workers; begins exhibiting at the Ferargil Gallery and then at the Maynard Walker Galleries in New York City; marries Anne Kutka in Santa Fe; moves to Eugene in November to begin teaching at the University of Oregon

1935
Morning Exercise, an oil painting, is reproduced in the August issue of *Art Digest*

1936
Spends time painting in Saugatuck, Michigan, where Francis Chapin was teaching at the AIC's summer school; McCosh would spend several more summers there in the following years

1937
Teaches summer courses at the AIC; "A Critical Appreciation of Iowa Painter David J. McCosh" by Edward Beatty Rowan and a reproduction of *I've Got a Toothache*, a drawing, are printed in *Magazine of Art*

1938
Installs *Incidents in the Lives of Lewis and Clark* mural in the post office in Kelso, Washington, as a Works Progress Administration commission; *Mill Race,* an oil painting, is reproduced on the title page of *Art News*

1939
January, Oregon, a watercolor painting, is reproduced in *American Painting Today* by the American Federation of Arts

1940
Installs two *Themes of the National Parks* murals for the National Parks Service in the Department of the Interior, Washington, D.C.

1942
Installs *Spirit of Beresford* mural in the post office in Beresford, South Dakota, as a Works Progress Administration commission; *Logged Off*, a watercolor painting, is reproduced in *Fortune* magazine

1947
Teaches at Montana State University in Bozeman during the summer

1949
Takes a sabbatical leave from the University of Oregon for one academic year to paint at Cohasset Beach, Washington, San Miguel de Allende, Mexico, and New Mexico

1954
Elected member of the American Watercolor Society and is made full professor of art at the University of Oregon

1956
Teaches painting workshop in Klamath Falls, Oregon

1957
: Serves as guest artist at San Jose State College, California, during the summer

1958
: Takes a sabbatical leave from the University of Oregon to paint in England, France, Italy, Morocco, and Spain

1962
: Illustrates Ernest G. Moll's poem "The Lightless Ferry" for publication in *The Rainbow Serpent and Other Poems*

1965
: Takes a sabbatical leave from the University of Oregon to paint in New Mexico and in San Miguel de Allende, Mexico City, and the Yucatan

1970
: Retires from teaching as professor emeritus

July 25, 1981
: Dies in Eugene, Oregon

While a member of the faculty at the University of Oregon, McCosh maintained an active schedule of regional and national exhibitions, including numerous entries in the "Annual All-Oregon Exhibition" at the Portland Art Museum (1934–35, 1940, 1942, 1946, 1952), "Paintings by Artists West of the Mississippi" at the Denver Art Museum (1935–37, 1940, 1945, 1955, 1956), and the "Annual Exhibition of Northwest Artists" at the Seattle Art Museum (1935–37, 1940, 1948, 1954–55). His sabbaticals to Washington, New Mexico, Mexico, and Europe were instrumental in his artistic development, and his mature work was intrinsically tied to his observations of nature. After his retirement from the University of Oregon, he continued to paint and exhibit until shortly before his death.

Along with the collections represented in this exhibition, McCosh's work is also owned by the Portland Art Museum, the Hallie Ford Museum of Art, the Seattle Art Museum, the Whitney Museum of American Art, and several other institutions and private collectors. Major retrospectives were held at the University of Oregon Museum of Art in1985, the Littman Gallery at Portland State University in 1986, and again at the University of Oregon Museum of Art in 1993 ("David McCosh Exhibition Series") and 2000 ("Community Favorites from the David McCosh Collection").

This publication is made possible with the generous support of The David John McCosh and Anne Kutka McCosh Memorial Museum Endowment Fund.

Issued in conjunction with the exhibition of the same title held July 23–September 4, 2011, Jordan Schnitzer Museum of Art, Eugene, Oregon.

Library of Congress Cataloging-in-Publication Data

McCosh, David, 1903–1981.
The Making of David McCosh: Early Paintings, Drawings, and Prints, July 23–September 4, 2011 / Danielle M. Knapp, McCosh Fellow Curator.
p. cm. Published in conjunction with an exhibition held at the Jordan Schnitzer Museum of Art, Eugene, Oregon.

ISBN 978-0-87114-096-8

1. McCosh, David, 1903–1981—Exhibitions.
I. Knapp, Danielle. II. Jordan Schnitzer Museum of Art. III. Title.
N6537.M39637A4 2011, 759.13—dc23, 2011022670

Published by
JORDAN SCHNITZER MUSEUM OF ART
1430 Johnson Lane
1223 University of Oregon
Eugene, Oregon 97403-1223
541.346.3027
jsma.uoregon.edu

Danielle M. Knapp, Editor
Diane Nelson, Designer
Printed by Premier Press, Portland, Oregon
Photography by Jonathan B. Smith and Malina Graves
Mark Tade, pp. 8 and 25; Tim Thayer, pp. 17 and 24; Smithsonian American Art Museum, p. 26